M000285158

RESILIENT

RESTORING YOUR WEARY SOUL IN THESE TURBULENT TIMES

STUDY GUIDE | FIVE SESSIONS

JOHN ELDREDGE

Harper*Christian*
Resources

Resilient Study Guide
© 2022 by John Eldredge

Requests for information should be addressed to:
HarperChristian Resources, 3900 Sparks Dr. SE, Grand Rapids, Michigan 49546

ISBN 978-0-310-09704-4 (softcover)
ISBN 978-0-310-09720-4 (ebook)

All Scripture quotations, unless otherwise noted, are taken from the Holy Bible, New International Version®, NIV®. Copyright © 1973, 1978, 1984, 2011 by Biblica, Inc.® Used by permission. All rights reserved worldwide.

Scripture quotations marked ESV are taken from The Holy Bible, English Standard Version. ESV® Text Edition: 2016. Copyright © 2001 by Crossway Bibles, a publishing ministry of Good News Publishers.

Scripture quotations marked MSG are taken from THE MESSAGE. Copyright © 1993, 2002, 2018 by Eugene H. Peterson. Used by permission of NavPress. All rights reserved. Represented by Tyndale House Publishers, a Division of Tyndale House Ministries.

Scripture quotations marked NASB are taken from the New American Standard Bible®, Copyright © 1960, 1971, 1977, 1995, 2020 by The Lockman Foundation. All rights reserved.

Scripture quotations marked NKJV are taken from the New King James Version®. Copyright © 1982 by Thomas Nelson. Used by permission. All rights reserved.

Scripture quotations marked NLT are taken from the Holy Bible, New Living Translation. Copyright © 1996, 2004, 2015 by Tyndale House Foundation. Used by permission of Tyndale House Ministries, Carol Stream, Illinois 60188. All rights reserved.

Any internet addresses (websites, blogs, etc.) and telephone numbers in this study guide are offered as a resource. They are not intended in any way to be or imply an endorsement by HarperChristian Resources, nor does HarperChristian Resources vouch for the content of these sites and numbers for the life of this study guide.

All rights reserved. No portion of this book may be reproduced, stored in a retrieval system, or transmitted in any form or by any means—electronic, mechanical, photocopy, recording, scanning, or other—except for brief quotations in critical reviews or articles, without the prior written permission of the publisher.

Published in association with Yates & Yates, www.yates2.com.

HarperChristian Resources titles may be purchased in bulk for church, business, fundraising, or ministry use. For information, please e-mail ResourceSpecialist@ChurchSource.com.

First Printing September 2022 / Printed in the United States of America

CONTENTS

Introduction v

SESSION 1: The Strength That Prevails 1

SESSION 2: Glory or Desolation 27

SESSION 3: Unconverted Places 53

SESSION 4: The Deep Well Inside Us 75

SESSION 5: Don't Look Back 101

Leader's Guide 127

Endnotes 135

INTRODUCTION

The fall itself took only seconds.

Four climbers, roped together, were descending from the summit of Mount Hood on May 30, 2002, using ice axes and crampons. They had finished the grueling five-hour climb with high-fives at the summit, and now it was time to get off the mountain. For some reason, they had decided to pull their fixed protection—their anchor of safety—and were attempting to walk down while roped only to one another, a string of weary men held to the ice by the tiny points of their crampons.

The top man slipped and fell. With thirty-five feet of rope between him and the climber below, he dropped seventy feet before the rope went taut—the equivalent of falling off a seven-story building. He was going at least thirty miles per hour when he yanked the second man off, and the speed and force multiplied from there with irreversible consequence. All four climbers were ripped from the mountain. As they plummeted toward the crevasse, the swirling tangle clotheslined two more teams of climbers, sweeping them all into the abyss. Three climbers died that day.

Why would they descend in such a risky manner? As Laurence Gonzales writes in *Deep Survival*:

> Most climbers reach the summit tired, dehydrated, hypoxic, hypoglycemic, and sometimes hypothermic. Any one of those factors would be enough to erode mental and physical abilities. Put together, they make you clumsy, inattentive, and accident-prone. They impair judgment.[1]

Tired decision-makers equals dangerous decisions.

But we already know that. We see the proof all around us. We entered the pandemic of 2020 already worn out by the madness of modern life.

Now, this series isn't about the pandemic, though when history tells our story, COVID-19 will be our generation's World War II—the global catastrophe we lived through. What began in 2020 was a shared experience of global trauma, and trauma takes a toll—the long experience of losses great and small; all the high-volume tension around masks, quarantines, vaccines, school closures; and on and on the list goes.

Journalist Ed Yong won the 2021 Pulitzer Prize for Explanatory Reporting for his coverage of the pandemic. Here's what he found:

> Millions have endured a year of grief, anxiety, isolation, and rolling trauma. Some will recover uneventfully, but for others, the quiet moments after adrenaline fades and normalcy resumes may be unexpectedly punishing. When they finally get a chance to exhale, their breaths may emerge as sighs. "People put their heads down and do what they have

to do, but suddenly, when there's an opening, all these feelings come up," Laura van Dernoot Lipsky, the founder and director of the Trauma Stewardship Institute, told me. . . . "As hard as the initial trauma is," she said, "it's the aftermath that destroys people."[2]

Right now, we're in a sort of global denial about the actual cost of these hard years (which are not over). We just want to get past it all, so we're currently trying to comfort ourselves with some sense of recovery and relief. But folks, we haven't yet paid the psychological bill for all we've been through. We would never tell a survivor of abuse that the trauma must be over now that the abuse has stopped. And yet that mentality is at play in our collective denial of the trauma we've been through.

We need to be kinder to our souls than that. Denial heals nothing, which is why I'm more concerned about what's coming than what lies behind. In our compromised condition, we're now facing some of the trials Jesus warned us about as we approach what the Scriptures refer to as "the end of the age" (Matthew 24:3).

In this hour, we don't need inspiration and cute stories. We need a survival guide—which is exactly what this study is designed to be.

The point is this: how are you going to adjust your life for recovery and resilience? You can't just slog on, burning everything you have to sustain what you think you ought to be doing. A time like ours requires real cunning. So don't let your weariness drag you right off the mountain. Make the decision to change your daily routines to develop a resilient soul.

If you want resilience, you'll do it. Survivors are flexible; they adapt to the changing environment around them—like being open to the supernatural graces and making them a normal part of life.

Let's come back to the climbing accident on Mount Hood and why those men made such a dangerous decision. The problem with climbing (I've been a climber for many years) is that we make the summit the goal. Making it to the top is the victory. This is the objective we obsess about weeks before the event. It's the prize we have in front of us as we undertake the rigors of the ascent. The climbers on Mount Hood that fateful day made the mistake of thinking the summit was the end of their mission, and they dropped their guard. But of course they were only *halfway* to their goal. The real finish line is safely down—your car in the parking lot, or your bed at home.

For the followers of Jesus, the real finish line is either the return of Jesus or our homecoming to him. *That's* why we cultivate endurance!

This study guide is a companion to my book *Resilient*. You can do the series as part of a group or on your own. Either way, you'll want to have a copy of the book and access to the video series, which are available via streaming (see the instructions provided on the inside of the front cover). You will note the book has ten chapters, and this is a five-session study guide, so some chapters of the book have not been included due to space. That's why we highly recommend reading the book in full in addition to being part of this study.

If you're leading a group, a guide has been provided for you in the back of this study. Each session in this guide follows this format:

- » Welcome
- » Core Scripture
- » Video Teaching
- » Group Discussion
- » Closing Prayer
- » Between-Sessions Personal Study (five days)
- » Recommended Reading (for the next session)

Each session will pull your attention to Jesus himself, while the practical skills throughout will revive your exhausted heart and mind. The peace and hope provided in Christ is always available to you—and his resilience never fails.

John

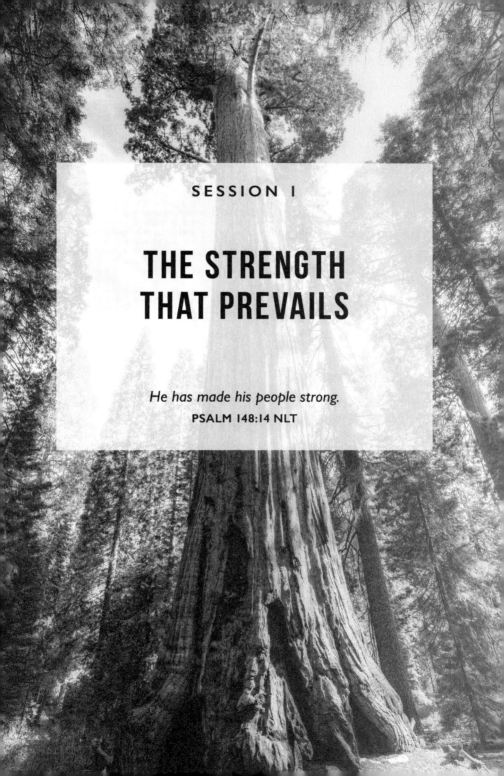

SESSION 1

THE STRENGTH
THAT PREVAILS

He has made his people strong.
PSALM 148:14 NLT

WELCOME

Welcome to session 1 of *Resilient*. This first session includes material from the Introduction, "No Ordinary Moment," and chapter 1, "I Just Want Life to Be Good Again," of the book. If there are new members in your group, take a moment to introduce yourselves to one another before watching the video. We suggest you simply share your name, some brief details about your life, and why you decided to join this study. Now, let's get started!

CORE SCRIPTURE

Invite someone to read aloud the following passage. Listen for fresh insight and share any new thoughts with the group through the questions that follow.

> *God raised [Jesus] from death and set him on a throne in deep heaven, in charge of running the universe, everything from galaxies to governments, no name and no power exempt from his rule. And not just for the time being, but forever. He is in charge of it all, has the final word on everything. At the center of all this, Christ rules the church. The church, you see, is not peripheral to the world; the world is peripheral to the church.*
>
> — EPHESIANS 1:20–23 MSG

» Story is the way we orient ourselves in the world. What story are you telling yourself—is it a political, social justice, economic, or some other narrative? Share the story that's seemed most real to you lately.

» As Ephesians 1:20–23 reminds us, the story of God is still the story of the world. Is that hard for you to believe . . . or hang onto in chaotic times? Explain.

» Does your current emotional state reflect your confidence that Jesus is absolute Lord of everything on earth, galaxies to governments? That his church is center stage, not the world? That Christ gets the final word? If not, why not?

VIDEO TEACHING

Play the video segment for session 1 (see the instructions provided on the inside front cover on how to access the video at any time via streaming). A summary of the key points is provided for your benefit as well as space to take additional notes.

Summary

In this five-part series, we' are going to discover essential skills for your survival in these turbulent times. *Resilient* is your guide for emerging from global trauma with your faith and your soul stronger than ever.

Toward the end of his days on earth, Jesus began to give his disciples clear instructions for living through extremely hard times, knowing they would record those instructions for future generations—including you, dear ones. He assured us in no uncertain terms that this story would sweep toward a climax and that those days would be especially hard on the human soul. He urged us to ask for the strength that prevails:

> *Keep alert at all times. And pray that you might be strong enough to escape . . . and stand before the Son of Man.*
> — LUKE 21:36 NLT

Strong enough to escape—that's who and what we want to be. Strong enough to be the survivors, the triumphant ones. To make it through the storm.

This is no ordinary strength Jesus is offering. This isn't optimism. This isn't simply feeling refreshed for a new day.

Hard times require something more than willpower. Jesus warns us, urges us, practically commands us, to ask for strength. The Greek word used here is *katischuó*, and it means

to be strong to another's detriment;
to prevail against;
to be superior in strength;
to overcome;
to prevail.[3]

Yet in these unprecedented times, we find ourselves continually having to "rally" to one crisis after the next—pandemics, financial challenges, wars and rumors of wars, job losses, and constant fear and grief. As we do, we are tapping deep into our soul's reserves. At some point, we must replenish those reserves, or we will burn out. But how do we choose real restoration over momentary relief when we can barely make it through the day?

In this first session, you will receive biblical insights, practical skills, and prayer to help you:

» tap into the supernatural graces that God promises to believers;
» understand the times through the parables of the fig tree and the ten bridesmaids;
» not let your reserves run dry;
» receive from Jesus the strength that prevails;
» experience supernatural resilience; and
» ask God to fill you with his River of Life.

Notes

GROUP DISCUSSION

Take a few minutes to go through the following questions with your group.

1. What stood out most from the opening adventure story of Wilfred Thesiger's impossible trek through the desert? Why?

2. The past several years have been times of severe testing on both global and personal levels. How would you describe your current mental, emotional, and spiritual state as you begin this study?

3. In Luke 21:29–36, Jesus offers an illustration of the fig tree to prepare us for the trials for an hour like this one. What advance council does he give for the strength to escape the madness of these times?

en we
the signs
no that the
dom of God
near!'s

When you see the g signs I have written & told you of; know my words are true & will not go away.

4. The Greek word for strength is *katischuó*. What three traits are reflected by this word?

5. What does the olive oil represent in the parable of the ten bridesmaids found in Matthew 25:1–10? What can we learn from the foolish bridesmaids about the dangers of running out of the very thing our souls most need? → *intimacy*

The oil represents intimacy, knowing Jesus, time spent w/ Him -- the investment of time w/ Him as wise, not foolish & last minute. Through parables He warns us to be & make ourselves ready. There wont be time to build yourself up & to replenish your soul when moment happen — You

6. According to 2 Chronicles 16:9, what type of people is God actively searching the earth for . . . and what does he promise to give them? How is this essential for your resilience?

must ahead of time NOW!

A heart thats loyal to Him
e promises to show Himself strong on their behalf.
His presence.
us is essential for my resilience as no fear can set it, love, peace, joy & more will be near me... Keeping me anchored to Him

CLOSING PRAYER

Receiving the Strength That Prevails

We are going to explore a number of "supernatural graces" as we move through this study. It will help your faith to know that your experience of these will be gentle. Though we call them "supernatural" graces, it doesn't mean they come like an earthquake or lightning strike. God is tender with our weary souls; he doesn't overwhelm us with his presence.

How do we tap into *katischuó*, the strength that prevails? It starts with what I like to call being singlehearted. We are singlehearted when we cherish God above all things. We love him in the longing for relief, which is where we are vulnerable. We love him in the longing for life to be good again. Scripture promises that God will come to the help of those who are singlehearted: "The eyes of the LORD search the whole earth in order to strengthen those whose hearts are fully committed to him" (2 Chronicles 16:9 NLT).

As we turn our hearts toward Jesus or our Father (they are one), we practice loving him. *I love you, God. I love you, God. I love you, God.* This is not *feeling* love—the warfare and the weariness will often make us feel rather blank. But we choose to love God anyways. This is the strength that prevails, giving us the first step of courage to stand and be singlehearted.

Over and over again, we practice loving God. *I love you, Lord.* And we ask him for *katischuó*—his overcoming, prevailing, conquering strength. God offers it, so ask, ask, ask!

If you're doing this study with a group, ask someone to read this closing prayer aloud. If you are going through this on your own, find a quiet space where you can speak the words aloud.

Father, Jesus, Holy Spirit—God of all creation, God of the thunderstorm and the waterfall, I need your strength. I need the strength that prevails. I don't want to fall away; I don't want to lose heart. I choose you above all things. I give you my allegiance and my undivided love. I choose single-heartedness toward you, Lord Jesus—body, soul, and spirit; heart, mind, and will. I pray for a supernatural resilience, God. Fill me with your overcoming strength, a victorious strength. Father, Lord of heaven and earth, strengthen me. I pray for strength of mind, strength of heart, strength of will. I pray for the strength that allows me to escape all that is coming against the saints in this hour. Fill me with resilience. By faith I receive it and thank you for it. In Jesus' name, amen.

That's a great beginning. Consider making this prayer something you turn to frequently in the coming week.

> To go deeper, try the program
> "30 Days to Resilient"—free within the
> One Minute Pause App.

GET

BETWEEN-SESSIONS PERSONAL STUDY

In this section, you're invited to further explore the mate-rial in *Resilient*. If you haven't already done so, read the Introduction, "No Ordinary Moment," and chapter 1, "I Just Want Life to Be Good Again," in the book at this time. Each day's study in this section offers a short reading from the book along with reflection questions designed to take you deeper into the themes of the study. Journal or just jot a few thoughts after each question. At the start of the next session, there will be a few minutes to share any insights . . . but remember that the primary goal of these questions is for your personal growth and private reflection.

Day One: NO ORDINARY MOMENT

Camels have an Achilles' heel; this is where we will begin.

But their vulnerability is hidden by their legendary *resilience*: these famous "ships of the desert" have been crossing dune seas since before the time of Abraham.

The stamina and strength of camels is truly impressive—they can carry heavy loads across leagues of burning desert sand, going without water for weeks while their human companions die of thirst. But the treacherous thing about camels is that they will walk a thousand miles with seemingly endless endurance, giving you little indication they are about to collapse. Then it just happens. As the Alchemist said to Santiago:

> Camels are traitorous: they walk thousands of paces and never seem to tire. Then suddenly, they kneel and die. But horses tire bit by bit. You always know how much you can ask of them, and when it is that they are about to die.[4]

Human souls hide an Achilles' heel too.

We have an astonishing capacity to rally in the face of calamity and duress. We rally and rally, and then one day we discover there's nothing left. Our soul simply says, *I'm done; I don't want to do this anymore*, as we collapse into discouragement, depression, or just blankness of soul.

You don't want to push your soul to that point.

But *everything* about the hour we are living in is pushing our souls to that very point. Some folks are nearly there.

Extraordinary times can be thrilling, but they also tend to be very demanding. Our hearts will need guidance and preparation. It would be a good idea to take the strength of our soul seriously at this time. We've got to plan for our recovery and find new resilience.

"At least we can get back to our normal lives," one friend said. But that's not true either. I know we all *want* it to be true, but events are converging that prevent normal life from happening. Our enemy, the prince of darkness, has engineered this situation to do serious harm to the human heart. I believe we are set up for a sweeping loss of faith.

There is hope, great hope. Jesus Christ knew that humanity would face hard times, especially as history accelerates toward the end of the age. He gave us counsel on how to live through such trials, and now would be a good time to pay attention to what he said. The Creator and Redeemer of our humanity has given us a path toward recovery and resilience. We would be fools to ignore it or push it off to "some other time."

Whatever you believe about the coming years, I think we can all agree that greater resilience of heart and soul would be a very good thing to take hold of.[5]

1. How are we similar to camels when it comes to resilience—both in helpful and dangerous ways?

helpful - we preservere, have hope. to get to destination (better, to live, etc.)

dangerous - we dont stop, rest, get away sleep, refuel, replenish, talk to others our real feelings, evaluate ourselves w/ the Lord

13

2. Have you experienced a time where you rallied well during times of calamity only to suddenly realize you were done with nothing left to give? What happened next—did you fall into discouragement, depression, or just blankness of soul? Explain.

> almost/sometimes – yes blankness

3. During these current chaotic times, why is not wise to put your hope in things just getting back to normal?

> Because there isn't a normal, normal has gone away. Normal distracts us from being singlehearted for Jesus. Normal will fade/crumble but the Father & His word is true forever.

Day Two: THE PRIMAL DRIVE FOR LIFE

The longing for things to be good again is one of the deepest yearnings of the human heart. It has slumbered in the depths of our souls ever since we lost our true home. For our hearts remember Eden.

How we shepherd this longing—so crucial to our identity and the true life of our heart—how we listen to it, but also guide it in right or wrong directions, determines our fate.

The epicenter of our being is the deep longing to *aspire* for things that bring us life, to *plan* for those things, to take *hold* of them, to *enjoy* them, and start the cycle over as we aspire toward new things! This is the essential craving for life given to us by God. Let's call this capacity the "Primal Drive for Life."

Our Primal Drive for Life has taken a real beating over the past few years.

It isn't only the pandemic. We were all running like rats on a wheel *before* 2020—addicted to technology, overwhelmed by global news, wrung out from social tensions, exhausted body and soul from the madness of modern life. Does anybody even remember? Life was *draining*. It wasn't like we stepped out of a three-year sabbatical when we stepped into 2020. We were set up to be steamrolled by the pandemic.

Then came the repeated cycles of fear, control, chronic disappointment, all those losses great and small, the inability to make plans for the future. This throttled our capacity for living, just as serial rejection harms our ability for relationship or chronic failure cripples our capacity for hope. We started reaching for relief.

Stasi and I were among the sixty-two *million* homeowners who did renovations during the pandemic. That's more than three-quarters of all homeowners in the US, the highest levels ever seen. We painted the living room, got new carpet, new chairs. We upgraded our garden as well. This was far more than boredom or the desire for change; it was a profound longing for a fresh start *at life* in the midst of so much loss and uncertainty. The renovation craze reflected something deeper—a yearning for life to be good again, expressed in paint and carpet, gardens and landscaping.

But the whole time Stasi and I were renovating our home, I could feel something was off. The preoccupation of making our home nicer took my mind off the death count in New

York, London, Paris, and Delhi, and the vicious acrimony over vaccines. But it didn't feel like the answer. It was good; I enjoyed it. But it didn't bring about the fix I was longing for.

Speaking of fixing things, I noticed through the first half of 2021 that I was doing all sorts of obsessive fixing. Everything from a dripping faucet to a lamp that had been wobbly for years—they each seized my attention, and I had to set it right. My soul was desperate to set things right. Haven't you felt this too?

Then life began to return to some semblance of normal—we got restaurants back, movies, outdoor concerts. The world rushed out like the starving survivor of a shipwreck brought back from isolation and set before a Sunday brunch. In the summer of 2021 you couldn't get a rental car, Airbnb, or campsite. Airports, beaches, and national parks were jammed. It was like spring break in Miami. The longing for things to be good again was (and is) raging.

Personally, I couldn't get enough. But all those comforts and activities weren't delivering whatever my soul was desperately longing for.[6]

I. How would you define the "Primal Drive for Life"?

The desire to see hopes, dreams,
cycle of life lived, fullfilled,
experienced as a p life passage.
H.S. > college > Married > Grandchildren
Travel > enjoyment w/ friends &
family. Work success & growth

2. What are the specific ways your heart longs for life to be good again? Do you sense these comforts and activities are capable of bringing your soul deep and lasting joy?

(To get back on track w/ #1 answers.)
→ No. Because they can be altered, taken away, not lasting joy.

3. When the world leaves you overwhelmed and exhausted, where do you turn for relief? Does doing so result in restoration or ultimately leave you feeling emptier?

I pray but not enough. Movies, food, feeling emptier.

Day Three: RESERVES

One of the most surprising things about human beings is how all that resilience can evaporate in a moment. One day the resources we have to sustain the Primal Drive for Life simply run out. The mother who for decades pours and pours into her family, and then one day up and has an affair with her best friend's husband. The minister who for decades served up banquets from the Word of God suddenly decides he doesn't believe in Jesus anymore.

It has to do with *reserves*.

We tap into our deep reserves to endure years of suffering and deprivation. We might feel like we're doing pretty well on any given day, but we're still burning through precious resources, and our reserve tank is precariously low.

This is the trauma cycle. We rally in the face of harm, and when the harm subsides, we live in denial of it and go off in search of some taste of Eden. When our efforts are thwarted, rage surfaces—which is common to trauma responses.[7]

This is why rallying can actually be deceptive. Reserves tell the true story.

Consider this: If another pandemic were to sweep across the globe next week, some brand-new deadly threat, and we found ourselves back to quarantines, living under the vague threat of suffering and death, in a state of constant uncertainty about the future, with no clear view of the finish line—how would your heart respond?

Or try this on: Your house or apartment is going to burn down tomorrow, and though everyone will survive, you will lose everything else. All your belongings, records, valuable documents, precious family keepsakes. You will need to rebuild your entire life. Do you have 100 percent vim and verve for that scenario?

Like I said—we have not yet paid the psychological bill for the COVID-19 pandemic. We tapped deep into our reserves to rally, and we are in no condition to face more trauma . . . let alone the assaults of our enemy. Trauma sensitizes you to more trauma and brings to the surface *past* trauma. You don't get used to it; each new crisis simply piles on the stress.[8]

The treacherous thing about human nature is that the Primal Drive for Life is so compelling that we will sacrifice almost anything for it—health, marriages, careers, even our faith. After a time of global trauma and deprivation, the longing rages, so we wander off in search of life. But reckless wandering without a clear plan or destination often adds to our suffering rather than bringing us relief.

When John Wesley Powell made the first descent of the uncharted Colorado River through the Grand Canyon in 1869, he and his colleagues had no idea of the test that was in store. Wild rapids, unexpected falls, swirling pools that threatened to devour their wooden boats. After weeks of this, several of the crew mutinied. Against all warnings, they left the river and tried to find an exit out of the canyon through Apache lands.

Those men were never heard from again.[9]

I fear we are being lured into similar dangers as we grasp for relief from all we have endured.[10]

I. Where would you say your reserves are on a scale of I to I0, with I0 being a full tank and I being empty? Why? *what I I dont know. why? Because feel can be changed when put in the situation & I'm not sure.*

2. Can you describe a recent time where you've gone through a trauma cycle? What initiated it and what was the outcome?
reading this book, initiated by describing what we went through outcome disgust, irritability & anger.

ow does the story of John Wesley Powell and his crew's fatal decision to mutiny reveal the danger of recklessly wandering in search of life with no plan?

Day Four: RETURN TO ME

The exodus of the people of Israel and their journey through the Sinai desert is one of the greatest survival stories of all time. More than two *million* people wandering through a land of sand and barren rock, homeless, looking for the land of abundance, a place to call home. When will life be good again?[11]

There were no real sources of food in that desert. Water was about as scarce as it is on the surface of the moon. A "barren wilderness—a land of deserts and pits, a land of drought and death, where no one lives or even travels" (Jeremiah 2:6 NLT).

This is more than a moment in Jewish history. It is recorded for us as one of the great analogies of human experience, our journey from bondage to freedom, from barrenness to the promised land. Ultimately, it is the precursor to our journey of salvation, from the kingdom of darkness to the kingdom of God.

It is a story about the Primal Drive for Life—where will we take our thirst?

This is *the* choice, *the* test. Always has been, always will be. This Primal Drive for Life was so compelling it caused thousands of those rescued slaves to mount a rebellion to go back to bondage in Egypt just to have their familiar ways back. Sobering.

> *"The heavens are shocked at such a thing and shrink back in horror and dismay," says the* Lord. *"For my people have done two evil things: They have abandoned me—the fountain of living water. And they have dug for themselves cracked cisterns that can hold no water at all!"*
>
> — JEREMIAH 2:12–13 NLT

The great alarm the Scriptures are sounding is that our longing for life to be good again will be *the* battleground for our heart. How we shepherd this precious longing, and *if* we shepherd it at all, will determine our fate in this life and in the life to come.

This is playing out in a "postpandemic" world: we only sort of want God; what we *really* want is for life to be good again. If God seems to be helping, awesome. We believe! If he doesn't . . . well, we'll get back to him later, after we chase whatever we think will fill our famished craving.

The first stage of the coming storm is this: we've all run off to find life and joy following years of stress, trauma, and deprivation. But it isn't working; *it won't ever work.* We return to our normal Monday through Friday disappointed, and disappointment will become disillusionment. And disillusionment makes us extremely vulnerable to our enemy.

We must lovingly shepherd our famished thirst back to the source of life.[12]

1. The Jeremiah 2:12–13 passage describes God's people as rejecting both his presence and his provision of living water. In the Primal Drive for Life, where do you take your famished craving?

2. In this post-pandemic world, do you really want life to be good again, but only sort of want God? What is a recent example where you experienced this?

3. How has your disillusionment with life made you vulnerable to the enemy's attacks?

Day Five: THE RIVER OF LIFE

When the human heart and soul experience month after month of disappointment and loss, death rolls in. Dr. Richard Gunderman described the progressive onset of disillusionment as the accumulation of hundreds or thousands of tiny disappointments, each one hardly noticeable on its own.[13] The loss of hope and dreams suffocates the Primal Drive for Life.

But our God has provision for us!

I know, I know—most of you think that what you need right now is three months at the coast. Walking on the beach, drinks on the deck, and with all my heart I hope you find that. But for most of us, a sabbatical in some gorgeous refuge is not available. What *is* available is the River of Life, God himself, in ways we have not yet tapped into.

God wants to make his life available to you. Remember—he's the creator of those beautiful places you wish you could go to for a sabbatical. All that beauty and resilience, all that life comes from God, and he wants to impart a greater measure of himself to you! The life of God is described in Scripture as a river—a powerful, gorgeous, unceasing, ever-renewing, ever-flowing river.

Ezekiel was given a number of beautiful visions, glimpses into the kingdom of God that permeates this world. He saw the temple of God in Jerusalem, and out of the temple was flowing the River of Life. As it flowed forth across the countryside, it became so deep and wide it wasn't possible to swim across it—an image of abundance! I love how the passage ends: "Where the river flows everything will live" (Ezekiel 47:9).

Everything will live. This is what we want—to live, to find life in its fullness again.

The apostle John was given a revelation of the coming kingdom and the restored earth, and he saw the River of Life flowing right down the middle of the city of God:

Then the angel showed me the river of the water of life, as clear as crystal, flowing from the throne of God and of the Lamb down the middle of the great street of the city. On each side of the river stood the tree of life, bearing twelve crops of fruit, yielding its fruit every month. And the leaves of the tree are for the healing of the nations.

— REVELATION 22:1–2

There is so much life flowing from God that it flows like a mighty river. Isn't that marvelous? Follow me now—the River of Life is not just for later. Jesus stated clearly that the river is meant to flow out of our inner being right here, in *this* life: "Let anyone who is thirsty come to me and drink. Whoever believes in me, as Scripture has said, rivers of living water will flow from within them" (John 7:37–38).

The mighty life of God flowing in you, and through you, saturating you like a river.

Now, let me pull all this together. We have a capacity and drive in us for living. It's a precious longing, and it's taken a beating. God is "the fountain of life" (Psalm 36:9). There is so much life flowing from God that it flows like a river no one can even swim across—a superabundant out- flow of life! This life is meant to flow *in* us, and *through* us.[14]

I. Be honest: which sounds more appealing to your weary heart right now—three weeks at your favorite vacation spot or God's River of Life? Why?

2. How might it change your heart and your resilience to have the mighty life of God flowing in and through you, saturating you like a river?

3. Jesus offers this invitation: "Let anyone who is thirsty come to me and drink. Whoever believes in me, as Scripture has said, rivers of living water will flow from within them" (John 7:37–38). Have you taken Jesus up on this invitation? If not, would you consider asking him to fill you now?

RECOMMENDED READING

Before your group gathers for the next session, read chapter 4, "Eden Glory, Not Desolation," in the book *Resilient*. This chapter will be the focus of session 2. Use the space provided to write any key points or questions you want to bring to the next group meeting.

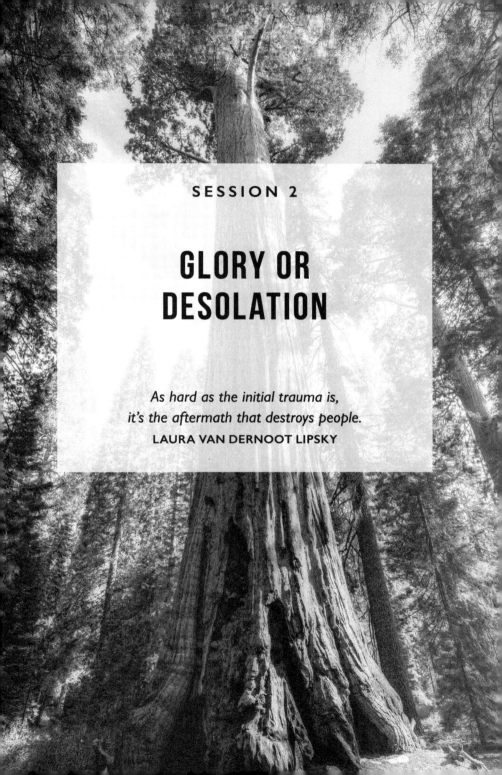

SESSION 2

GLORY OR DESOLATION

As hard as the initial trauma is,
it's the aftermath that destroys people.
LAURA VAN DERNOOT LIPSKY

WELCOME

Welcome to session 2 of *Resilient*. This second session includes material from chapter 4, "Eden Glory, Not Desolation," of the book. If there are new members in your group this week, take a moment to introduce yourselves to one another before watching the video. We suggest you simply share your name, some brief details about your life, and why you decided to join this study. Also, share any insights from last week's personal study. Now, let's get dive in!

CORE SCRIPTURE

Invite someone to read aloud the following passage. Listen for fresh insight and share any new thoughts with the group through the questions that follow.

When I think of all this, I fall to my knees and pray to the Father, the Creator of everything in heaven and on earth. I pray that from his glorious, unlimited resources he will empower you with inner strength through his Spirit. Then Christ will make his home in your hearts as you trust in him. Your roots will grow down into God's love and keep you strong.

— EPHESIANS 3:14–17 NLT

» In these chaotic times, it appears resources are scarce and we're all running on empty. How does that contrast with the two words used to describe God's resources?

» God will empower us with inner strength through his Spirit. How does it feel that this strength isn't up to us? What must our roots grow deep in to keep us strong?

» When we trust in Christ, where does he make his home? What does this say about the nearness of Jesus to us at all times?

VIDEO TEACHING

Play the video segment for session 2. A summary of the key points is provided for your benefit as well as space to take additional notes.

Summary

You've probably seen one of those nature documentaries at some point in your life—magnificent cinematography showing thousands of caribou migrating across the tundra, or wildebeest making their annual pilgrimage across the Serengeti.

Sweeping down from high above, the camera first shows us a myriad of animals all moving in a vast wave, then zooms in closer to discover a small member of the herd lagging behind as the narrator explains, "The injured calf is now dangerously separated from the herd." You don't even need to guess what's coming next. Wolves. Hyenas. I hate that part about nature; the world can be a violent place.

Jesus knows that very well, personally.

The urgency with which he sometimes pleads, urges, and warns us is born out of a profound sobriety. Wander away from your Shepherd and you will encounter harm. The forces of darkness come "to steal and kill and destroy" as he bluntly put it (John 10:10). Oh that we would take this more seriously than we do. What would the camera show if it panned down over our lives today to reveal what is stalking us?

One thing's certain. You we would move closer to the Shepherd.

But in our weary condition we just want flip-flops and mai tais, so we don't pay careful enough attention.

As Jesus began to explain the trials of the final hours, the urgency of his warnings increased:

"You will be hated by everyone because of me, but the one who stands firm to the end will be saved."

— MATTHEW 10:22

"The one who stands firm to the end will be saved."

— MATTHEW 24:13

"By your endurance you will gain your lives."

— LUKE 21:19 ESV

Endurance—the dividing line between those who make it through any sort of trial and those who don't. Hang on, don't get discouraged—this isn't just gutting it out. Not at all. The beautiful resilience Jesus offers us comes from *his* resources; endurance is *imparted* to us.

In this second session, you will receive biblical insights, practical skills, and prayer to help you:

- » describe the symptoms of Desolation that is raging throughout the world;
- » reveal where God has relocated his temple;
- » explain why the heart is the epicenter of our story;
- » explore the regenerative, resurrecting Eden Glory of God;
- » practice supernatural graces that overcome shortage and deprivation; and
- » invite the Eden Glory of God into your being.

Notes

GROUP DISCUSSION

Take a few minutes to go through the following questions with your group.

1. The tragic opening story of Timothy Treadwell reveals that the world is a dangerous place. Do you live with that awareness? How so?

2. In Matthew 24:13, Jesus says: "The one who stands firm to the end will be saved." On a scale of 1 to 10 (with 10 being best), how are you faring now in terms of standing firm? Share why.

3. What impact has Desolation had on you in the past few years?

4. What does Ezekiel 36:26 say about our hearts? Is this a new revelation or something you grew up being taught? Explain.

5. In Ephesians 3:17, Paul says that Christ will make his home in your heart. What does that mean in terms of what your heart now represents?

6. How would you describe the Eden Glory of God—not in religious language but in everyday language that stirs your soul?

CLOSING PRAYER

Receiving the Eden Glory of God

As we discussed in the first session, we are going to be exploring a number of "supernatural graces" as we move through this study. Remember, even though we are calling them "supernatural" graces, it doesn't mean they come like an earthquake or lightning strike. God is tender with our weary souls; he doesn't overwhelm us with his presence.

Give this simple prayer, asking for the Eden Glory of God, a try throughout this week. You'll see. Once again, if you're doing this study with a group, ask someone to read this closing prayer aloud. If you are going through this on your own, find a quiet space where you can speak the words aloud.

Father, Jesus, Holy Spirit, I receive your Glory into my being. I receive the Glory that fills the oceans, the Glory that sustains the sun. I receive the Glory that raised Christ from the dead! I pray that your Eden Glory would fill my heart, soul, mind, and strength. I am your temple, Lord; come and fill your temple with your Glory! I also pray that your Eden Glory would shield me against all forms of Desolation coming over my life. I renounce every agreement I might have made with Desolation, every agreement large and small. I choose you, God. I renounce the Falling Away, and I choose you. Regardless of how I feel, I choose you, Lord. You are my God and Savior. I pray that your Eden Glory would fill my life—restoring me, renewing me, granting me supernatural endurance and resilience. I also invoke your Eden Glory over my life as a shield, over my household and domain. I invoke your glory, love, and kingdom as my constant strength and shield. In the name of the Lord Jesus Christ, ruler of heaven and earth. Thank you, Lord!

This prayer has become so important to me I find myself invoking the phrase, "Your glory, your love, your kingdom," all throughout my day.

To go deeper, try the program
"30 Days to Resilient"—free within the
One Minute Pause App.

BETWEEN-SESSIONS PERSONAL STUDY

In this section, you're invited to further explore the material in *Resilient*. If you haven't already done so, read chapter 4, "Eden Glory, Not Desolation," in the book at this time. Each day's study in this section offers a short reading from the book along with reflection questions designed to take you deeper into the themes of the study. Journal or just jot a few thoughts after each question. At the start of the next session, there will be a few minutes to share any insights . . . but remember that the primary goal of these questions is for your personal growth and private reflection.

Day One: THE SUPERNATURAL GRACES

Amphibians are creatures that can live in two worlds.

Christians are likewise designed to live in and enjoy the benefits of two worlds, ecosystems, two realities—the physical and the spiritual, the earth and the heavens.

Each world offers graces for human flourishing. The natural world is saturated with beauty, and beauty nourishes the human soul. That's why we vacation in lovely places—when we're looking to be renewed, we choose walks in the woods, swimming in the ocean, biking through vineyards, music, and dinner on the patio under the stars. There are many natural graces that nourish and strengthen the heart and soul—beauty is one, stillness is another, and so are nature and disentangling from technology.

We are also created to live comfortably in the *spiritual* world, to draw upon the supernatural graces available to us through the rest of God's wonderful kingdom.

If you've ever experienced the comfort of God, or the love of God, that was heaven coming to you here on earth. You tapped into the rest of God's kingdom for the help, strength, and sustenance you needed.

Prayer is reaching into the heavens for what we need. If you have had the joy of hearing Jesus speak to you, if he brings to you Scriptures, songs, things that stir your heart, that's the heavens coming into your natural world. You are tapping into the resources of God's kingdom. And there is *so* much more to discover!

For some reason, I'm thinking of penguins. They aren't technically amphibians, but they move comfortably between two worlds. Like most mammals that live on land, they nest on land, sleep on land, mate on land, raise their chicks on land. But they are wonderfully adept in the ocean. Penguins are, in fact, awkward on land, but they are so graceful, even elegant, as they swim and dive in the water. We are meant to be the same: not only adept but even elegant in our ability to swim in the rest of God's kingdom.

Our created nature is designed to live in two worlds, drawing our strength from two worlds; that's why I call us amphibians. But most of us are not tapping into the super-natural graces. We can't ignore these and hope to thrive in an hour like this one. If you place a frog—a true amphibian—in a tank of water with no dry place to crawl onto, it will die. If you place it in a terrarium with no water, it will die. Amphibians need both realms to thrive. We cannot hope to find resilience while we ignore the provision God has for us in the fullness of his beautiful kingdom.[15]

1. Christians are designed for two ecosystems—the physical and the spiritual. Why do you think most believers have settled for living only in the physical realm?

2. Are you comfortable spending time in the spiritual realm and experiencing its benefits? Why or why not?

3. What supernatural graces—Scriptures, songs, or prayer practices—help you tap into the resources of God's kingdom?

Day Two: DESOLATION

I suffered a couple of devastating emotional blows in the summer of 2021. There were things I felt God had promised me that, in heartbreaking ways, did not come through. I felt so betrayed, so abandoned. But then, in my vulnerable state, something came over me—a dark cloud, a sort of suffocating fog that urged me to give up my life with God.

I shared my experience with two colleagues of mine, godly men with a long history of relationship with Jesus. They confided that they, too, had experienced something exactly like my Desolation. In fact, both of them had gone through an episode in the spring of 2021 where they felt that they might entirely lose their faith. Given their resilience, I was shocked. It seemed absurd that such solid men of faith could come to that place.

What's important about all three of our stories is that once each of us came out from under this fog, and our life with God was back to normal, everything was fine again. While there were genuine human disappointments involved, the sudden onset and dramatic relief from this fog revealed that it was from the enemy, tied directly to the Falling Away predicted for this hour. The common symptom was a Desolation of heart and soul, which sure seems tied to something Jesus warned us about (see Matthew 10:22; 24:13; Luke 21:19).

The prophet Daniel foretold a day when "the one who makes desolate" would step onto the world stage (Daniel 9:27 NASB). This was prophesied as part of the final trials of the age. Jesus referred to this same reality in his own warning and counsels. Paul went on to link this force—whatever it may be—to the Falling Away he spoke of in 2 Thessalonians 2:3: "Let no one deceive you by an means, for that Day will not come unless the falling away comes first" (NKJV).

We don't need to get into labyrinthine debates over the Antichrist, the Beast, the whore of Babylon, and how all that might play out on the world stage. There's no need to go down that rabbit hole to simply acknowledge that something or someone is going to cause Desolation, and that Desolation is part of what causes people to give up on God. This is something we most definitely want to strengthen our hearts against. My colleagues and I have experienced it, and we've seen it in our clients and constituents around the world.

The symptoms include a sort of dullness of heart, a poverty of spirit, a barrenness of soul. Disappointment, so understandable given the circumstances, collapses into disillusionment. Neither hope nor joy comes easily.

Worst of all, there comes a kind of blankness in our life with God. Faith feels flat, or dumb, or simply . . . gone. We are disappointed with God, and we feel we don't believe in him anymore. Hopelessness infects our faith. Like the limping caribou, we're beat up and lagging behind, vulnerable to the predators that want to drag our souls into Desolation. Trust me—you do not want to fall prey to this. It's terrible.

We must find the supernatural graces to guard our hearts against both Desolation, whatever the source, and the riptide pull to draw away from God—or even to give up on God entirely.

Because the battle is over the heart, my friends. Always. The battle is over your heart.[16]

1. Have you recently struggled with deep disappointment, disillusionment, a lack of hope and joy, or even a loss of faith? How could identifying these feelings as symptoms of Desolation help you interpret what is really going on?

2. How can Desolation, if unaddressed, erode one's resilience and relationship with God?

3. What supernatural graces or practices might be helpful in guarding your heart and soul against Desolation?

Day Three: THE TEMPLE OF YOUR HEART

Desolation, whatever it may be, is linked in the Scriptures to defiling the temple of God. Because of this, many Christians assume that the temple in Jerusalem needs to be rebuilt for these last-days prophecies to come true.

But folks, have we forgotten that God relocated the temple? In a stunning shift of geography, God changed the playing field. He moved the temple from a physical building to the hearts of his people:

> *Don't you know you yourselves are God's temple and that God's Spirit dwells in your midst?*
> — 1 CORINTHIANS 3:16

> *God's temple is sacred, and you together are that temple.*
> — 1 CORINTHIANS 3:17

> *For we are the temple of the living God.*
> — 2 CORINTHIANS 6:16

> *Do you not know that your bodies are temples of the Holy Spirit, who is in you, whom you have received from God?*
> — 1 CORINTHIANS 6:19

You, dear child of God, follower of Jesus, are now the temple. The New Testament makes that clear. Follow this closely, because it is so very holy, so deeply encouraging, and it will bring you vital resilience for this hour. Your heart is the dwelling place of the Almighty! (If you've invited him in,

43

which is easy to do. You simply say, "Lord Jesus—I need you. I really do. I open the temple of my heart to you; I ask you to come and dwell within me. I surrender my life to you in every way. Come and be my saving God, dwelling in my heart.")

In the Old Testament, first came the tabernacle and then the temple. These were holy places where God came to be among his people:

> Then the cloud covered the tent of meeting, and the glory of the LORD filled the tabernacle.
>
> — EXODUS 40:34

> Then the temple of the LORD was filled with the cloud . . . for the glory of the LORD filled the temple of God.
>
> — 2 CHRONICLES 5:13–14

No wonder Satan tried on *multiple* occasions to defile, desecrate, and ultimately destroy both tabernacle and temple—for here was the epicenter of the life of Israel with their saving God. Here God met with his people.

But at the coming of Jesus Christ—Immanuel, God with us—the abiding place of the Holy One shifted in a breathtaking way. When Christ died on the cross, the veil of the temple in Jerusalem was torn top to bottom; the Holy Spirit came down on Pentecost; and now the temple has moved location to the human heart, because that is where God comes to dwell "that Christ may dwell in your hearts" (Ephesians 3:17).[17]

Our enemy knows God has set up a new temple—the heart of his people.[18] So he tries to bring Desolation there. Satan is trying to defile the hearts of God's followers, because this is where the holy of holies now lies. (Here on earth, anyways; there is the true place in heaven.)[19]

1. In the Old Testament, the dwelling place of God was in the tabernacle and later in the temple. According to 1 Corinthians 3:17, where is the new temple?

2. How does this relocation of the temple change our access to— and relationship with—God?

3. The enemy has constantly tried to bring Desolation to God's temple. How does this attack on the temple now impact every believer . . . including you?

Day Four: THE COMING STORM

One of the infamous consequences of COVID is the loss of taste and smell. For some people this symptom carries on for many, many months. The daughter of a friend of ours is a bright, musical, vibrant fifteen-year-old who, like her family, loves fantastic foods from around the world. Her particular favorite is Korean food. But she lost her sense of taste with COVID and *one year later* still hasn't gotten it back. She lost the joy of eating. Now, anyone can handle that for a week or two, but when it goes on for a year, it feels like it will go on forever. This is such vulnerable territory, a place where Desolation can get in and take root.

We still don't know the long-term effects of all this, but it looks like up to a third of all cases are long-haul COVID, lasting more than six months.[20] I've had friends whose symptoms lasted more than a year. This wears down whatever remaining resilience we may have, making us vulnerable to Desolation in many forms—especially disappointment with God and pulling away from him.

Laura van Dernoot Lipsky is the founder and director of the Trauma Stewardship Institute. She has spent decades helping people navigate the consequences of natural disasters, mass shootings, and other crises. "As hard as the initial trauma is," she said, "it's the aftermath that destroys people."[21]

This is the coming storm I am most concerned about. Every therapist I know in the US and Europe has a long waiting list; this is the mental health crisis catching up with us. God our Father knew we were going to have to live through such times, and he has made provision for us.[22]

1. Look again at the quote from Laura van Dernoot Lipsky: "As hard as the initial trauma is, it's the aftermath that destroys people." What aftermath are you or a loved one currently going through that is based on a prior traumatic event?

2. Has the aftermath proven to be even more difficult than the original event? Why or why not?

3. After years of global trauma, the long-term effects will happen as millions simultaneously grapple with the aftermath. How can resilience help you weather this coming storm?

Day Five: EDEN GLORY

When you think of what Desolation looks like, picture a barren desert. Desolation wants to make everything a wasteland.

So, what is the opposite of a wasteland?

Eden! The paradise of God, our first home, with all its lush, glorious beauty overflowing here, there, everywhere!

If you follow the flow of Scripture and human history, you can see that our enemy wants to make everything a wasteland, and God wants to make everything a restored Eden. When it comes to the resilience we need against Desolation, part of our Father's provision is his Eden Glory—the glory of God in you and around you, giving you supernatural resilience and guarding you like a shield.

What do I mean by Eden Glory?

Think of the wedding at Cana, where Jesus turned water into wine. Christ had the attendants fill six stone jars with water. Each jar could hold up to thirty gallons. Then Jesus turned every drop into wine—and fine, sumptuous wine at that, the kind of wine you'd expect to find in Eden, or at the wedding feast of the Lamb! One hundred eighty gallons of exquisite wine poured into the party at the end of the evening. (Jesus is the kind of person you want to hang out with, by the way; he knows how to bring joy to any occasion!)

After telling that story, John wrote, "What Jesus did here in Cana of Galilee was the first of the signs through which he revealed his glory; and his disciples believed in him" (John 2:11).

What exactly did Jesus reveal? God's supernatural power to overcome shortage and deprivation with overwhelming abundance! That's his glory; he did it by the power of his glory.

In the book of Romans, Paul is trying to help us understand the availability of the power of God for us, in us. He turned to the resurrection and said, "Just as Christ was raised from the dead through the glory of the Father, we too may live a new life" (Romans 6:4). It was by the glory of God that Jesus was raised from the dead. The glory of God—the regenerative, resurrecting Eden Glory of God.

Isaiah reminds us that "the whole earth is full of his glory" (Isaiah 6:3). Think of the sun, how absolutely wonderful the sun is! Its radiance, beauty, and cheerfulness, and how much life it gives! It is pulsating with the glory-power of God. Think of the oceans and the forests of the world, how vast they are, how filled with life. The whole world is filled with the glory of God. It is the life-giving, life-sustaining, *generative power* of God.

So, for our purposes here, when you think of the glory of God, think of the sun, the ocean, water turned into wine, Christ raised from the dead. Think of Eden.

Now for something truly breathtaking: you are meant to be filled with the glory of God.

Think back to the tabernacle and temple—in the Old Testament, the glory of the Lord filled the tabernacle, then the temple. The manifest presence of God came and dwelt there, filled with radiance, beauty, and regenerative power. Remember, you are now the temple. The New Testament makes that clear. This is why Paul wrote:

> *But we all, with unveiled faces, looking as in a mirror at the glory of the Lord, are being transformed into the same image from glory to glory, just as from the Lord, the Spirit.*
>
> — 2 CORINTHIANS 3:18 NASB

The transformation of your character and the regeneration of your humanity is taking place in you *because of the glory of God in you*! (How else could it take place?) The New International Version adds, "with ever-increasing glory."

We need the Eden Glory of God—the regenerative, life-giving, life-sustaining glory of God—in great measure right now. We need a greater measure of the manifest presence of Jesus in us. And we are *meant* to be filled with it. The glory of God is meant to fill our hearts and souls. So by all means, let's ask for this supernatural grace![23]

1. In the flow of Scripture and human history, our enemy wants to make everything a wasteland, and God wants to make everything a restored Eden. What might it look like for the barren places within your life to be restored with Eden Glory?

2. Isaiah says that "the whole earth is full of his glory" (Isaiah 6:3). What examples of God's glory do you see in the world today?

3. Can you describe a time when the glory of God has given you supernatural resilience and guarded you like a shield? If not, will you ask God to fill your heart and soul with his Eden Glory now?

RECOMMENDED READING

Before your group gathers for the next session, read chapter 6, "Unconverted Places," in the book *Resilient*. This chapter will be the focus of session 3. Use the space provided to write any key points or questions you want to bring to the next group meeting.

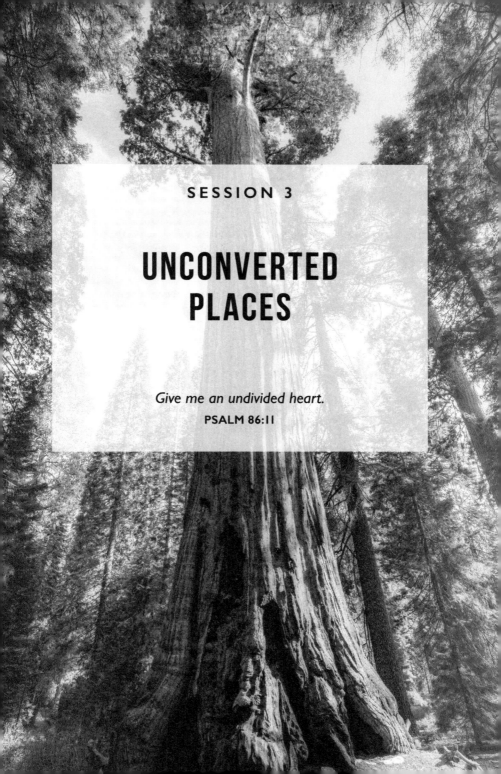

SESSION 3

UNCONVERTED PLACES

Give me an undivided heart.

PSALM 86:11

WELCOME

Welcome to session 3 of *Resilient*. This second session includes material from chapter 6, "Unconverted Places," of the book. If there are new members in your group this week, take a moment to introduce yourselves to one another before watching the video. We suggest you simply share your name, some brief details about your life, and why you decided to join this study. Also, share any insights from last week's personal study. Now, let's get started!

CORE SCRIPTURE

Invite someone to read aloud the following passage. Listen for fresh insight and share any new thoughts with the group through the questions that follow.

Now Peter was sitting out in the courtyard, and a servant girl came to him. "You also were with Jesus of Galilee," she said.

But he denied it before them all. "I don't know what you're talking about," he said.

Then he went out to the gateway, where another servant girl saw him and said to the people there, "This fellow was with Jesus of Nazareth."

He denied it again, with an oath: "I don't know the man!"

After a little while, those standing there went up to Peter and said, "Surely you are one of them; your accent gives you away."

Then he began to call down curses, and he swore to them, "I don't know the man!" Immediately a rooster crowed.

— MATTHEW 26:69–74

» Survival stories bring out the best and worst in people. What does this story reveal about Peter's inner struggle in this moment?

» Who we are, what we love, and how far we are willing to trust God are revealed when we are truly hard pressed. Where have you seen this play out in your own life?

» During trying times, it is the unconverted places in our lives that will prove our downfall if we don't bring them to Christ. What "pockets of resistance" do you sense that Jesus wants to go after to strengthen your resilience?

VIDEO TEACHING

Play the video segment for session 3. A summary of the key points is provided for your benefit as well as space to take additional notes.

Summary

As Jesus began to explain the trials of the final hours, he warned us several times about hatred, and how hanging on to love will prove very difficult: "And many will turn away from me and betray and hate each other. . . . Sin will be rampant everywhere, and the love of many will grow cold" (Matthew 24:10, 12 NLT).

Wow. If this doesn't describe our times, I don't know what does. You can't express one single opinion online without receiving poisonous retaliation. Humanity is raw and angry (there's the trauma at work). Hatred is ruining all public discourse. Love grown cold.

Following the global trauma of 2020, I noticed something emerging in the traffic of our neighborhood. Two distinct drivers began to appear. There were the timid drivers, who would stop for eternal periods at intersections before proceeding. Then there were the ragers, the folks who would fly up behind me (because they were going twenty miles per hour over the speed limit) and ride my bumper as if they wanted to drive right through me until they had a chance to pass. Both fear and rage are part of the trauma response, and there's lots of it out there now.

I am among them, though my rage behind the wheel looks far more self-righteous. I *hate* it when the ragers ride someone dangerously close, then pass them in a place they should never try passing. If I'm the guy they are bearing down upon I will slow down even more, forcing them back under the speed limit. But the hatred in my heart is still hatred just the same.

We are hard-pressed, folks, and we aren't exactly shining.

It is our inner weaknesses, brokenness, and frankly the "unconverted places" that are going to take our legs out from under us.

Maturity is no longer optional, dear ones; wholeheartedness is no longer something we can go without. Those vulnerabilities in us prove treacherous in this world, like a faulty bridge or a bow that is not properly strung.

In this third session, you will receive biblical insights, practical skills, and prayer to help you:

- » expose the pockets of resistance within you;
- » unveil the sweet safety of holiness;
- » expose the Comfort Culture's substitute goals;
- » embrace wholeheartedness;
- » permeate your being with the presence of Christ;
- » deal with your vulnerabilities; and
- » ask God to convert the unconverted places within you.

Notes

GROUP DISCUSSION

Take a few minutes to go through the following questions with your group.

1. As the Mount Everest story reveals, crisis exposes who we are. Did the selfish actions of the two climbers surprise you? Why or why not?

2. Do you agree with the descriptions of the two kinds of drivers since the traumatic events of 2020? How has it affected your driving—and reaction to other drivers?

3. Salvation is a process, not an event. While our homecoming is utterly life-changing, it's not instantaneously life-changing. What are your thoughts on this?

4. What most stands out to you about Eustace's transformation in the passage read from *The Voyage of the Dawn Treader* by C. S. Lewis? Why?

5. Paul writes in 1 Thessalonians 5:23, "Now may the God of peace make you holy in every way, and may your whole spirit and soul and body be kept blameless until our Lord Jesus Christ comes again" (NLT). How will this keep you resilient during times of severe testing?

6. The Comfort Culture offers countless other goals than the pursuit of holiness. Do you feel a pull to that—or to become the most converted person your friends and family know? Explain.

CLOSING PRAYER

Converting the Unconverted Places

At the close of the video, and in chapter 6 of the book, I walk through the steps of this skill in more detail. It's one you'll want to spend time in throughout the week.

In this prayer, I am not suggesting that the existence of unsanctified places in us means that we have lost the security of our homecoming to God. Not at all. But salvation is also a re-creation, and in this sense we are not yet his here.

For now, let's close with this simple prayer. If you're doing this study with a group, ask someone to read this closing prayer aloud. If you are going through this on your own, find a quiet space where you can speak the words aloud.

Oh Jesus, I pray for the salvation that is truly salvation. I don't merely want to be forgiven; I want to be truly saved . . . permeated by Christ. Here I am. I open up the unconverted part of me to you, Lord. Save me here. I pray that you would have all of me, the good and the bad. I surrender every unconverted place in me to you, to your indwelling presence. I give this part of my life to you, Lord. I give this part of my humanity to you. Save me here. Unite with me here; permeate me here. I pray to be completely converted here. Jesus, unite with every part of me that is not yet united with you. Integrate my entire being into one, whole person united with you. I pray for complete union with you throughout my being. For you alone are my salvation, and I ask you for the salvation that is truly salvation right here. I ask for your holiness here. In your name.

To go deeper, try the program
"30 Days to Resilient"—free within the
One Minute Pause App.

BETWEEN-SESSIONS PERSONAL STUDY

In this section, you're invited to further explore the material in *Resilient*. If you haven't already done so, read chapter 6, "Unconverted Places," in the book at this time. Each day's study in this section offers a short reading from the book along with reflection questions designed to take you deeper into the themes of the study. Journal or just jot a few thoughts after each question. At the start of the next session, there will be a few minutes to share any insights . . . but remember that the primary goal of these questions is for your personal growth and private reflection.

Day One: THE SWEET SAFETY OF HOLINESS

"Now may the God of peace make you holy in every way, and may your whole spirit and soul and body be kept blameless until our Lord Jesus Christ comes again" (1 Thessalonians 5:23 NLT).

I absolutely love this verse; I love the hope of my entire being made pure by the Spirit of God.

I realize that *holiness* is a word with a lot of baggage for many people, but we can get past all that if we look at the gorgeous life and character of Jesus—he was simply good through and through. His character is so alluring, so winsome, and whenever you see him relating to people you are watching true holiness in action. Women who everyone had used and abused came to Jesus, threw themselves at his feet, and he was only loving toward them. Sometimes the crowds loved him, other times they shouted for his head, but he didn't let it faze him. Jesus' goodness in the Gospels is captivating.

When his own time of severe testing came, that goodness was his shield. Just before the secret police came for him, before the grisly scenes that follow, Jesus told his disciples, "I will no longer talk much with you, for the ruler of this world is coming, and he has nothing in Me" (John 14:30 NKJV).

The enemy tried every angle he could find on Jesus— seduction, rejection, threat, the fear of not having enough, even torture. Nothing worked, because Satan had nothing "in" Jesus to use as his hook. Imagine the sheer relief of it.

It probably feels like obtaining even a fraction of that goodness is beyond you, but the promise of the Christian faith is that God *will* reproduce Jesus' goodness in you: "I feel as if I'm going through labor pains for you again, and they will continue until Christ is fully developed in your lives" (Galatians 4:19 NLT).

The goal of God's work in us is Jesus taking up residence in every part of us. Nothing left out. No little pockets of resistance.[24]

I. *Holiness* is a word with a lot of baggage for many people. What baggage, if any, does it hold for you?

2. How does looking at the life and character of Jesus help you get past this baggage?

3. According to Galatians 4:19, what is the goal of God's work in you? How will this process get rid of any remaining pockets of resistance?

Day Two: COMFORT CULTURE

In our own times of severe testing, we want to be made "holy in every way," our entire "spirit and soul and body . . . kept blameless" (1 Thessalonians 5:23 NLT). Let me be quick to add, I think much of the testing and the Falling Away takes place very subtly in the heart. It's the small turns from God toward our other comforters, the quiet feelings of being disappointed with him, the early stages of Desolation—this is how most of the testing plays out. But it has momentum like an avalanche.

C. S. Lewis's personal secretary was a man named Walter Hooper. He described the Oxford professor and creator of Narnia as "the most thoroughly converted man I ever met."[25] What a wonderful thing to be said about you. Lewis was a man whose entire being—heart, soul, mind, and strength—had become almost thoroughly inhabited by Jesus Christ. His fragmented self was nearly fully reintegrated in Christ. (Nearly, because none of us are utterly whole until Christ returns. But my goodness—*nearly* is fabulous.) Many people fell in love with the presence of Dallas Willard for the same reason.

Let me pause on that thought for a moment, because while this is known to the saints, the Comfort Culture framed within us other goals. Does your heart tell you that it agrees with this—that the goal of your life is to become the most converted person your friends and family know?

Or does your heart prefer the goal to be something else? Perhaps, "I just want things to be good again, and let somebody else live through the end of the age"? Ouch. That hits close to home.[26]

1. In our times of testing, the goal is to be made "holy in every way," our entire "spirit and soul and body . . . kept blameless" (1 Thessalonians 5:23 NLT). What gets in the way of that in your life?

2. Initially, most testing plays out subtly in the heart but has momentum like an avalanche. What small turns from God toward other comforters have you been making over time?

3. What do you find most alluring about today's Comfort Culture? How might you pursue greater resilience here?

Day Three: "NOT HAVING OUR RATHERS THIS TRIP"

The battle taking place over the human heart can be described as Satan using every form of seduction and threat to take our hearts captive and our loving Jesus doing everything he can to form single-heartedness in us. This often plays out in thousands of small, daily choices. Which is kind, really; we want to develop single-heartedness *before* the severe testing comes.

Theodore Roosevelt had a lifetime of stories to prepare him for his last great adventure and ordeal—descending an unnavigated tributary of the Amazon in primitive canoes. And he needed preparation, because he nearly died on that trip. But this is the fellow who rode eighteen hours on horseback across the Dakota Badlands without water because the spring from which they'd planned to get water had dried up.

I love another story about a hunting trip during which Roosevelt and his guide repeatedly got their wagon stuck in mud as they tried to travel into the mountains.

> The second plunge of the horses brought them up to their bellies in the morass, where they stuck. It was freezing cold, with the bitter wind blowing, and the bog holes were skimmed with ice; so that we passed a thoroughly wretched two hours while freeing the horses and unloading the wagon.... My companion preserving an absolutely unruffled temper throughout ... whistling the "Arkansas Traveller." At one period, when we were up to our waists in the icy mud, it began to sleet and hail, and I muttered that I would "rather it didn't storm"; whereat he stopped whistling for a moment to make the laconic rejoinder, "We're not having our rathers this trip."[27]

A whole lot of that gets you ready for just about anything.

Maybe this helps you reinterpret the story of your own life. Maybe all those former hardships were developing resilience in you![28]

1. Jesus is doing everything he can to form single-heartedness in us while Satan is using every form of seduction and threat to take our hearts captive. How do you see this playing out in your life and those you love?

2. In the quote you read, when Theodore Roosevelt was up to his waist in icy mud, sleet, and hail trying to rescue his horses and wagon, he muttered that he would "rather it didn't storm." His companion famously replied, "We're not having our rathers this trip." What reaction do you have to this story?

3. Have you considered that all the past hardships you've faced may actually be developing resilience in you? How does that change how you interpret the story of your life?

Day Four: DEALING WITH OUR VULNERABILITIES

You've already lived through trying times. You already know quite a bit about what it means to be hard-pressed; what most people *don't* know is what to do with everything that has surfaced.

A man I counseled years ago, a Christian leader of deep integrity, wrote to me recently. He said, "I don't understand what's happening. I've never really entertained the possibility of an affair until now. But over the course of the last six months, I find myself battling that temptation and feeling like I'm losing the battle. I haven't surrendered but I don't understand what's going on in my heart."

The longing for things to be good again is making us vulnerable to all sorts of compromises. I can help you with this.

First, let's remove the shock and shame of those moments when hard-pressed you suddenly rages, binges, goes faithless, or simply shows up as a very unappealing version of you.

Salvation is a process, not an event.

Oh yes—salvation is a *homecoming* to be sure. That is the event. Our salvation begins when we first turn toward Jesus with an open heart. We come to him for mercy. We ask him to forgive us for living so much of our life utterly ignoring him. We invite him in as our rescuer. We also surrender; we yield the throne of our lives to him. That's the homecoming, and our Father is so absolutely giddy over it he wants to throw you a party. (In fact, the angels *did* party over your homecoming—see Luke 15.)

Our homecoming is utterly life-changing.

But what surprises us, what can really dishearten us, is that it's not *instantaneously* life-changing. Not thoroughly, that is. This is because salvation is also the re-creation of our fallen humanity, a restoration of our life through union with Christ. And that happens over time.

> *The way of the righteous is like the first gleam of dawn, which shines ever brighter until the full light of day.*
>
> — PROVERBS 4:18 NLT

> *For by one sacrifice he has made perfect forever those who are being made holy.*
>
> — HEBREWS 10:14

Note the process clearly laid out in these verses—dawn to day, cleansed and now being made holy.

But you already know this to be true; you're living out the process every day.

Parts of you seem well-inhabited by Christ. The rest of you seems practically pagan (revealed in your driving, bingeing, media choices, fantasy life, or the desire for life to be good again overwhelming all other faculties). How can these parts exist in the same human being? Because we are like stained glass—beautiful even in our brokenness, but made up of many fragments.

Everyone is fragmented.

Part of me loves God, confessed the apostle Paul, *and part of me rebels* (see Romans 7). This condition is why David cried out, "Give me an undivided heart" (Psalm 86:11). This is why salvation is a *process*, and it will help you be kind and merciful when those unconverted parts of you suddenly show up. Simply because the rage, bitterness, unbelief, or whatever pops out of the closet doesn't mean your salvation isn't real. It means parts of you are yet to be united to Christ. So let's talk about how to get them united with Jesus, because we are in dire need of the resilience that holiness provides.[29]

1. The longing for things to be good again makes us vulnerable to all sorts of compromises. How have you seen this play out in society? How has it played out in your life?

2. Everyone is fragmented. As Paul confessed, "I myself in my mind am a slave to God's law, but in my sinful nature a slave to the law of sin" (Romans 7:25). Where do you feel most fragmented?

3. Salvation is a *process*. This is why David cried out, "Give me an undivided heart" (Psalm 86:11). Are you kind and merciful to yourself when the unconverted parts of you suddenly show up? Why or why not?

Day Five: THE SALVATION THAT IS TRULY SALVATION

According to Jesus, "The Kingdom of Heaven is like the yeast a woman used in making bread. Even though she put only a little yeast in three measures of flour, it permeated every part of the dough" (Matthew 13:33 NLT).

Yeast gets into the dough and slowly works its way through the entire batch. The promise is this: the goodness of Jesus *will* work its way through your entire being. Jesus is the yeast, by the way—it is his gorgeous life living in you that begins to permeate your being and truly save you.

That is what salvation is: the permutation of your being by the presence of Christ in you, healing you, renewing you, imbuing you with his own life. Nineteenth-century Scottish author and minister George MacDonald wrote:

> The notion that the salvation of Jesus is a salvation from the consequences of our sins, is a false, mean, low notion. The salvation of Christ is salvation from the smallest tendency or leaning to sin. It is a deliverance into the pure air of God's ways of thinking and feeling. It is a salvation that makes the heart pure, with the will and choice of the heart to be pure.[30]

It follows, then, that what we are cooperating with, what we seek with all our hearts in this hard hour, is the process where God exposes some part of us *not yet* united to Christ, so that it *can* be united to Christ. This is the new way of looking at the stuff that emerges when you are hard-pressed.

This is why the military and those outdoor leadership programs have such good results—they provide for live, in-the-moment experiences of dealing with your stuff. But so does Christianity, and you don't even have to leave town.[31]

1. How do Jesus' words in Matthew 13:33 reflect the promise that his goodness *will* work its way through your entire being?

2. George MacDonald said the notion that the salvation of Jesus is a salvation from the consequences of our sins, is a false, mean, and low notion. What does he say that true salvation is?

3. A new way of viewing what emerges when you're hard-pressed is that God is exposing a part of you *not yet* united to Christ so it *can be* united to him. How might this approach help you gain greater resilience in real time?

RECOMMENDED READING

Before your group gathers for the next session, read chapter 8, "The Deep Well Inside Us," in the book *Resilient*. This chapter will be the focus of session 4. Use the space provided to write any key points or questions you want to bring to the next group meeting.

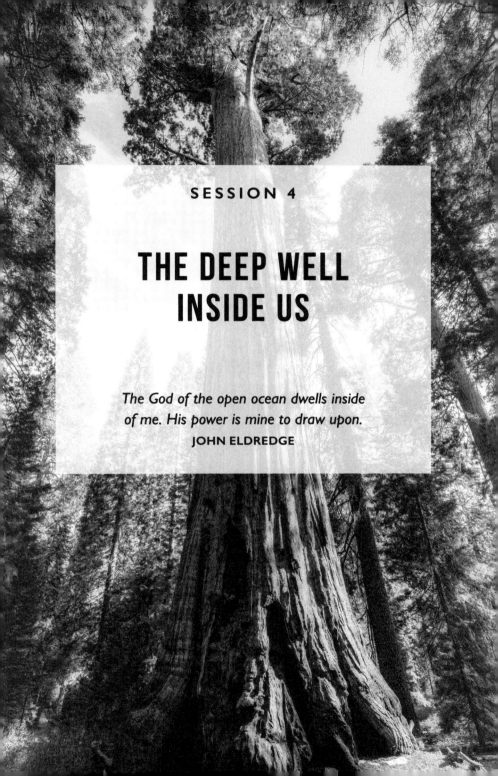

THE DEEP WELL
INSIDE US

The God of the open ocean dwells inside
of me. His power is mine to draw upon.
JOHN ELDREDGE

WELCOME

Welcome to session 4 of Resilient. This fourth session includes material from chapter 8, "The Deep Well Inside Us," of the book. Before you begin, take a few minutes to share any insights you had from last week's personal study. Now, let's get started!

CORE SCRIPTURE

Invite someone to read aloud the following passage. Listen for fresh insight and share any new thoughts with the group through the questions that follow.

Patient endurance is what you need now, so that you will continue to do God's will. Then you will receive all that he has promised.

> *"For in just a little while,*
> *the Coming One will come and not delay.*
> *And my righteous ones will live by faith.*
> *But I will take no pleasure in anyone who turns away."*

But we are not like those who turn away from God to their own destruction. We are the faithful ones, whose souls will be saved.
— HEBREWS 10:36–39 NLT

» What does this passage make clear that we need in this moment—and why does it say we need it?

» What is the fatal mistake that many will make in these latter days?

» Who are the faithful ones—and what are they promised?

VIDEO TEACHING

Play the video segment for session 4. A summary of the key points is provided for your benefit as well as space to take additional notes.

Summary

We are taking hold as best we can of the strength that prevails, the glory of God in us, so that we might have all we need to navigate these days victoriously. That strength—that beautiful, overcoming strength—comes from the source of life himself, from Jesus Christ who dwells within us. It makes sense, then, that we would practice turning our attention to Jesus *within* us, learning to draw from his strength in the depths of our being.

It's important we remember that the strength that prevails is a strength given to us by God. This is not something we conjure up. It's not gritting our teeth and doubling down. The strength we are after is a *supernatural* strength that rises up from the God who not only created us but dwells within us.

"God is the strength of my heart and my portion forever" (Psalm 73:26). How wonderful, how life-changing it is to experience God as the strength of your heart!

We are talking about the beauty, strength, and glory of the oceans, forests, waterfalls, thunderstorms—all the wild power of creation. This is the power of God made available to us. Imagine if that beauty, strength, and glory not only dwelt within you but also could be tapped into whenever you needed?

What if you could draw upon that glorious energy and power? It would change things for sure.

Every human being is actually a deep well. We just don't draw upon those places within us because we live near the surface of our own existence. The madness of the world around us, with its incessant carnival of distraction and demand, *is designed to keep us in the shallows.*[32]

We actually have three "levels" of being: the Shallows, Midlands, and Depths. The secret of all recovery and resilience is that, when invited, Jesus Christ himself comes to dwell within our created nature, deep down in the center of our being. And it is down in the depths that we must learn to tap into him for the strength that prevails.

In this fourth session, you will receive biblical insights, practical skills, and prayer to help you:

» grasp how essential endurance is at this time;

» tap into the supernatural strength from the God who created and dwells within you;

» understand the three "levels" of our being: the Shallows, Midlands, and Depths;

» learn to commune with God in the depths of your being; and

» descend through prayer to find Jesus-within-you.

Notes

GROUP DISCUSSION

Take a few minutes to go through the following questions with your group.

I. Can you relate to Colter Barnes' adventure story and his refusal to give up as he kept repeating the words, "I gotta dig deep; I gotta dig deep"? Explain.

2. We tend to think our strength is up to us, so we grit our teeth and double down—yet Psalm 73:26 says, "God is the strength of my heart and my portion forever." How does this verse reframe where the strength that prevails actually comes from?

3. Do you tend to spend more time in the Shallows, the Midlands, or the Depths? Why do you think that is the case?

4. When you pray, where does it seem God is located? Does he feel far away, next to you, or even closer? Explain.

5. What does Paul say in Ephesians 3:14–16 about where God is?

6. How can the prayer of descent help you tap into the presence of Jesus-within-you?

CLOSING PRAYER

Descending to Find Jesus-Within-You

What will you find as you find Jesus-in-the-depths-of-you? Friends, you will find such goodness, expressed personally to your need in that moment.

You are able to receive the strength that prevails as you commune with God's presence within you. His glorious resilience is always available. Simply lingering in the presence of Jesus-within-you strengthens you. Remember, just because these are supernatural graces doesn't mean they are dramatic. Receiving his love and strength is often a gentle experience.

If you're doing this study with a group, ask someone to read this closing prayer aloud. If you are going through this on your own, find a quiet space where you can speak the words aloud.

Start with this simple prayer. You'll notice some of the phrases are said several times. Repetition is really helpful in this kind of prayer. Here we go:

Jesus, I long for your presence, Lord. Help me commune with you where you live inside of me.

Jesus, I long for your presence, Lord. Help me commune with you where you live inside of me.

Jesus, I long for your presence, Lord. Help me commune with you where you live inside of me.

Jesus, I give everyone and everything to you, God.
I give everyone and everything to you.

Jesus, I give everyone and everything to you, God.
I give everyone and everything to you.

Holy Spirit, help me to descend.
Help me locate Christ in me.

Help me follow Christ down into the depths of my being. I pray to commune with you there.

I love you, God. I love you, God. I love you. I love you, God. I love you, God. I love you.

Father, Jesus, Holy Spirit, fill the depths of my being with your glory.

Fill me with your glory, Lord. Fill me with the river of life in my inmost being. Let the river flow in me. Give me the strength that prevails, Lord. Fill me with your glorious strength.

I pray for supernatural resilience. In your mighty name I pray.

To go deeper, try the program
"30 Days to Resilient"—free within the
One Minute Pause App.

BETWEEN-SESSIONS PERSONAL STUDY

I n this section, you're invited to further explore the material in *Resilient*. If you haven't already done so, read chapter 8, "The Deep Well Inside Us," in the book at this time. Each day's study in this section offers a short reading from the book along with reflection questions designed to take you deeper into the themes of the study. Journal or just jot a few thoughts after each question. At the start of the next session, there will be a few minutes to share any insights . . . but remember that the primary goal of these questions is for your personal growth and private reflection.

Day One: THE SHALLOWS, MIDLANDS, AND DEPTHS

I realize the idea of descending into the place where God dwells within us is probably new to most going through this study. It would *not* be new to the Christian monastic tradition for centuries, but most of us haven't had monastic training. So let's take it step by step; I think you'll discover this is quite accessible.

First, let's name the "levels" of our being:

> » You have fleeting thoughts throughout the day, most of which are insignificant.
> » You also have longings, hopes, and dreams that are far more important.
> » Deep within you, you have experienced the cry for love, hope, and joy, which feels almost primal to your being.

Everyone has a Shallows, a Midlands, and a Depths.

The Shallows of your being are characterized and ruled by the distractions of life. In the shallows your attention flits from thought to thought, distraction to distraction. What you want for lunch. The email you just read. A song from high school. Random thoughts flitting through your attention like a thousand butterflies. Those are the Shallows of your existence.

The Midlands are characterized and ruled by what I, echoing Jesus' words, would call "the cares of this life" (Luke 21:34 ESV): the deeper worries, heartaches, longings and aspirations that occupy the human heart. Things like the health of your aging parents, the learning struggles of your children, the progress of your career. When Jesus said, "Watch yourselves, lest your hearts be weighed down with . . . the cares of this life" (Luke 21:34 ESV), this is the geography of heartache and fear he was referring to.

But deeper still, down in the "depths of your being," is the essence of your existence and the dwelling place of God (now that you have invited him to live in you!). The Depths are characterized and ruled by eternal things like faith, hope, love, and joy, to name a few. The prisoner sentenced to solitary confinement, the patient living out the final days of life in a lonely hospital room, and the castaway stranded on a remote island all discover that what once seemed so important now pales in the light of their longing to see their loved ones one more time.

We all have a deep inner life, whether we pay attention to it or not. This is very hopeful, because we *can* learn to access it.[33]

I. The Shallows are characterized and ruled by the distractions of life. Have you realized how much of your day you spend in this "level"? What are ways you can intentionally spend less time in the Shallows?

2. The Midlands are deeper down in your being because they are the terrain of weightier matters such as your hopes and fears for your future or the future of your loved ones. What pressues from this "level" are weighing you down while keeping you up at night?

3. The Depths are where you access the essence of your existence and the dwelling place of God in you. How frequently do you find yourself here with God? How might more time in the Depths lead to greater resilience in every "level" of your life?

Day Two: HOW DO WE DESCEND?

We are looking to find the presence of God in our inmost being, to experience him and commune with him there. By tapping into his actual presence within us, we are able to receive the strength that prevails. It begins with simply giving him your attention. As Theophan the Recluse instructed, "One must descend with the mind into the heart, and there stand before the face of the Lord, ever-present, all-seeing, within you."[34]

This is one of those quotes that sounds all profound and spiritual . . . but we don't really know what he's talking about. It seems beyond our experience, but I don't think it needs to be. The key idea here is the descending part. We learn to drop down into the presence of God within us, tap into his strength there.

When Theophan instructed us to "descend with the mind into the heart," I think by our "mind" he was referring to our conscious attention, and by "heart" he meant our inmost being, the Depths.

The psalmist cried out to God from his innermost being; he then gave the fullness of his attention to God:

> *Out of the depths I cry to you, LORD;*
> *Lord, hear my voice.*
> *Let your ears be attentive*
> *to my cry for mercy. . . .*
>
> *I wait for the LORD, my whole being waits . . .*
> *I wait for the Lord*
> *more than watchmen wait for the morning,*
> *more than watchmen wait for the morning.*
>
> — PSALM 130:1–2, 5–6

Watchmen scan the horizon with careful attention; for their lives and the lives of the people within the city they protect depend on their attentiveness. The psalmist is using an analogy from his world to talk about *undistracted focus*: looking for God with all our attentiveness. It is something we give our whole being to. (You're going to love learning this, friends, and you're going to really love the fruit of it in your life.)

We set aside a time to give God our undivided attention (the battle is always for our attention). The new thought is that we are giving our attention to God-who-lives-within-us. As we tune out the world around us and tune in to our hearts, we become aware of the presence of Jesus-within-us. Take the experience of being comforted by God. Most of the time, nearly all of the time, that comfort is something we experience within. It might be facilitated by a comforting word or a passage of Scripture, but the comfort itself is taking place *within* us. There you go—you are tuning in to the work of God within you.[35]

1. Which phrase or thought from this psalm most resonates with you? Why?

2. The *watchmen* in the psalm represent an undistracted focus: looking for God with all our attentiveness and our whole being. What does the thought of giving God your undivided attention stir in you (longing, fear, joy, impossibility)? Why?

3. How does it feel to know you can regularly experience the comfort of God within you?

Day Three: CAST ALL YOUR ANXIETY ON HIM

Finding God always begins with loving him.

Just begin to love Jesus, or your Father, or the Holy Spirit within you. *I love you, God. I love you, God. I love you.* Settle in, knowing you are taking it slowly. *I love you, God. I love you, God. I love you.*

As we do this, we intentionally leave the distractions of the Shallows. We tune them out; we choose to ignore them. We begin to drop into our own being. As we consciously and intentionally love Jesus- within-us, it allows his Spirit to guide us into communion with him.

Because our attention is ruled 99 percent of the time by the Midlands and the Shallows, we have to get untangled from all that distraction to "descend." This is where benevolent detachment comes in—learning to give everyone and everything over to God. I explain this discipline in my book *Get Your Life Back*:

> We are aiming for release, turning over into the hands of God whatever is burdening us *and leaving it there*. It's so easy to get caught up in the drama in unhealthy ways, and then we are unable to see clearly, set boundaries, respond freely.[36]

"Cast all your anxiety on him because he cares for you" (1 Peter 5:7). We're looking for a way to take back some healthy detachment in our lives.

> You've got to release the world; you've got to release people, crises, trauma, intrigue, all of it. There has to be sometime in your day where you just let it all go. All the tragedy of the world, the heartbreak, the latest shooting, earthquake—the soul was never meant to endure this. The soul was never meant to inhabit a world like this. It's way too much. Your soul is finite. You cannot carry the sorrows of the world. Only God can do that. Only he is infinite. Somewhere, sometime in your day, you've just got to release it. You've got to let it go. . . .
>
> Benevolent detachment takes practice. . . . "I give everyone and everything to you, God. I give everyone and everything to you." Often, I find I need to follow that up with some specifics: "I give my children to you," for I worry about them. "I give that meeting to you." "I give this book to you." As you do this, pay attention—your soul will tell you whether or not you're releasing. If the moment after you pray you find yourself mulling over the very thing you just released, you haven't released it. Go back and repeat the process until it feels that you have.[37]

This isn't about attaining some new level of sainthood. We're simply pausing, and releasing, and as we get the hang of it, we really do get better at letting go and leaving it "let go."

Descending to find God within us is a good time to practice benevolent detachment, because in this moment we are not asking our souls to let go of everything forever, only to let go for a few moments of focused prayer. I suppose mature saints are able to do it as a matter of living, but for our purposes we practice in order to find God in the depths of our being.

We cast all our cares upon him, as 1 Peter 5:7 urges us. We let go, surrender control, and withdraw from the world by putting it all in the hands of God for a few moments.

Give everyone and everything to me. This is how Jesus began to teach me to let go. So I repeat that phrase right back to him as my way of cooperating. *I give* everyone *and everything to you, God. I give everyone and everything to you.* This allows me to move my attention down into the depths of my being.[38]

1. So many times, we make finding God an intellectual exercise. Yet today's reading states that "finding God always begins with loving him." What does that stir in you?

2. Your attention is ruled by the Midlands and the Shallows around 99 percent of the time. How will the practice of benevolent detachment (releasing everyone and everything to God) help you get untangled from all this distraction and "descend"?

3. First Peter 5:7 invites you to cast all your cares upon God. Where do you find it most difficult to let go and surrender control in your life? Why?

Day Four: WHERE IS THE GOD YOU'RE PRAYING TO?

Most of us are unpracticed at drawing anything from the depths of our being because the tumultuous, upset world we live in constantly pulls, pushes, and distracts us, moment by moment keeping us on the surface of our life with God. But with practice you can ignore all that and find the beautiful presence of Jesus-within-you. Notice when you're praying—where is the God you are praying to *located*?

Are you praying to the Lord of the heavens up above?

Are you praying to Jesus who is always with you, by your side?

Or are you praying to Jesus who now lives in the depths of your own heart? The God who resides within you?

If you are looking to dig for deeper resources, you'll need to look deep within. Saint John of the Cross wrote a lovely poem about an angel coming to a man in desperate straits. The angel led him to a forest, and at a certain place told him to dig. He found buried treasure. John ended the poem by having the angel say to us, "Dig here, in your soul."

We ask the Holy Spirit to help us:

The Spirit searches all things, even the deep things of God. For who knows a person's thoughts except their own spirit within them?

— 1 CORINTHIANS 2:10–11

The Spirit helps us in our weakness. We do not know what we ought to pray for, but the Spirit himself intercedes for us. . . . He who searches our hearts knows the mind of the Spirit, because the Spirit intercedes for God's people in accordance with the will of God.

— ROMANS 8:26–27

I pray something like this:

Holy Spirit, help me to descend.
Help me locate Christ in me.
Help me follow Christ down into the depths of my being.
I pray to commune with you there.[39]

1. When you pray to God, where do you sense he is? How does your response reveal your opportunity to enter into deeper communion with God?

2. The poem by Saint John of the Cross ends with the angel saying, "Dig here, in your soul." Do you believe God has deeper resources awaiting if you will look deep within? If not, what are the thoughts or doubts you are struggling with?

3. When we don't know how or what we should pray, the Spirit intercedes for us (see Romans 8:26–27). Will you write a simple prayer below, asking the Holy Spirit to help you to descend and to locate Christ in you?

Day Five: WHAT WILL YOU FIND?

Simply giving Jesus our lingering, undivided attention is going to be a new experience for most of us because we don't give *anything* our lingering, undivided attention these days. The following exercise itself will begin to strengthen your ability to command your attention, which is a good thing in itself. The practice builds mental resilience.

For me this began in this manner:

I would be in a simple time of prayer or quiet reflection, looking to give my attention to Jesus. As soon as I "found him" and tuned in to his presence with me, he would seem to recede from me. His presence seemed to draw back or draw deeper within. At first this was unsettling—why was my Lord retreating from my attempts to come close?

Rather than going to resignation and unbelief—that horrible little *I knew it* that resides in all of us—I asked him what was taking place. Jesus said, *Follow me.* Then I knew he was trying to get me to come deeper into my own being, to get out of the madness of the Shallows and the heartache of the

Midlands in order to find a deeper experience of his presence within me.

Be merciful with your efforts. Many times I've been in a moment of genuine communion with God-within-me when suddenly I'm yanked back to the Shallows by some distraction, or pulled to the Midlands by some care. Do not be distressed by this; it's very common. The entire world is shouting at you all the time, trying to capture your attention, and we are unfamiliar with lingering communion with God. Be kind to yourself by simply acknowledging, *Oh, I got yanked back to the surface.* And drop back down again.

What will you find, as you find Jesus-in-the-depths-of-you?

Friends, you will find such goodness, expressed personally to your need in that moment.

You will find love. Often your experience will simply be one of being loved, of knowing God's love for you. Linger with that; it is enough. (When I'm having a hard time "dropping in," I will often use the trail of love. I find where the longing for love lies within me, and I follow it to Jesus, like Hansel and Gretel following the breadcrumbs home. It leads to Jesus, who always lives in the place of love in our innermost being.)

Other times, Jesus has instructed me to find my longing for hope (again, never too far out of reach) and follow the longing for hope down into my inner being.

As we commune with God's presence within us, we are able to receive the strength that prevails. His glorious resilience is always available to us. Simply lingering in the presence of Jesus-within-us strengthens us. The communion is the point. Remember, just because these are supernatural graces doesn't mean they are dramatic. Don't look for fireworks and explosions. God is gentle. Receiving his love and strength is often a gentle experience.

Sometimes we find that God wants to say something to us, or show us something. Give him your attention.

Holy Spirit, help me hear what Jesus is saying to me.

Holy Spirit, help me see what Jesus is showing me.

I have had hundreds of beautiful encounters with Jesus through this practice. He has shown me the new earth. Seeing its beauty, seeing the utter victory of it was healing in itself and filled me with assurance. He has shown me the city of God, filled with laughter and joy. It increased my longing to be there.

Just go with what Jesus is doing; each experience tends to be unique.[40]

1. In the account you just read, when Jesus seemed to draw back, what was he actually doing? Does this give you a new interpretation for the times you thought Jesus was retreating from your attempts to come closer? Explain.

2. Receiving God's love and strength is often a gentle experience. Do you sometimes miss what he wants to say to you or show you because you expect fireworks and explosions? What is this revealing about your times of communion with God?

3. What do you most hope that you will find as you find Jesus-in-the-depths-of-you? Why is that your deepest longing?

RECOMMENDED READING

Before your group gathers for the next session, read chapter 10, "Hold On!," in the book *Resilient*. This chapter will be the focus of session 5. Use the space provided to write any key points or questions you want to bring to the next group meeting.

SESSION 5

DON'T LOOK BACK

"Remember Lot's wife! Whoever tries to keep their life will lose it, and whoever loses their life will preserve it."

LUKE 17:32–33

WELCOME

Welcome to our final session of *Resilient*. Congratulations! Well done. Really, well done! This is a big accomplishment that will prove beneficial for months and years to come. This fifth session includes material from the chapter 10, "Hold On!," of the book. Before you begin, take a few minutes to share any insights you had from last week's personal study. Now, let's get started!

CORE SCRIPTURE

Invite someone to read aloud the following passage. Listen for fresh insight and share any new thoughts with the group through the questions that follow.

> *When Lot still hesitated, the angels seized his hand and the hands of his wife and two daughters and rushed them to safety outside the city, for the LORD was merciful. When they were safely out of the city, one of the angels ordered, "Run for your lives! And don't look back or stop anywhere in the valley! Escape to the mountains, or you will be swept away!" . . .*
>
> *Lot reached the village just as the sun was rising over the horizon. Then the LORD rained down fire and burning sulfur from the sky on Sodom and Gomorrah. He utterly destroyed them, along*

with the other cities and villages of the plain, wiping out all the people and every bit of vegetation. But Lot's wife looked back as she was following behind him, and she turned into a pillar of salt.

GENESIS 19:16-17, 23-26 NLT

» Even when Lot hesitates, God made sure that he, his wife, and their two daughters made it safely outside the city. In spite of God's judgment on Sodom and Gomorrah, what attribute does he display to Lot's family in this action?

» There are pivotal moments in our lives where we face a fundamental test of our allegiance. What choice did Lot's wife make—and why did it have such a fatal implication?

» When discussing our trials at the end of the age, Jesus gives this sobering reminder: "Remember Lot's wife! Whoever tries to keep their life will lose it, and whoever loses their life will preserve it" (Luke 17:32-33). What does Lot's wife have to do with our predicament and the ageless battle for the human heart?

VIDEO TEACHING

Play the video segment for session 5. A summary of the key points is provided for your benefit as well as space to take additional notes.

Summary

Why did Lot's wife look back? She was warned by angels not to. Their stern, holy faces made it clear. Yet she looked back, *turned back* in her heart. Jesus said it had to do with her grasp for life to be good again (see Luke 17:32–33). She thought she would lose her life, everything she thought she needed for life, and she turned back.

This is far closer to us than we might think. You see, friends, all change initially feels like loss. When you leave one life to pursue another—a career change, a shot at grad school, even something as hope-filled as a new marriage—all you know is the life you are leaving behind. The adventure ahead is still strange and unknown, and thus you are more aware of what's behind than what's ahead. So it initially feels like loss.

This doubt, this fear, has crept into many good hearts in this hour. Which is why Jesus reminds us: Remember Lot's wife. This has to be one of the most cryptic, sobering, and, honestly, *unnerving* things Jesus ever said. Ever. The story of Lot's wife is a tragic tale of divided allegiance and the power of this world to trap the human heart. In spite of every pull this world gains over us, Jesus is urging us, *Do not look back. No divided hearts; no divided allegiances.*

God urges us to choose single-hearted commitment to him. To weather the coming storm, you need endurance and resilience. It's available in him. But it won't just happen. You must take hold of the strength that prevails.

So—what's your plan to make it through?

You need a plan, dear ones. Resilience and victory aren't going to come with a swipe on your home screen. Honestly, it can be as simple as this adjustment:

The world really has gone mad.
I'm not going to get pulled down with it.
I'm readjusting my life around recovery and resilience;
this is my orientation now.

In this final session, you will learn how to guard against divided allegiances by making recovery and resilience a regular practice. Above all, you will be discover how to create an ongoing plan that includes these two things:

1. **Renewing your love and devotion to Jesus:** Give time each day to loving him. This deepens your union and allows you to draw upon the life of Jesus-within-you. It's simple, but most folks don't even spend five minutes a day simply loving Jesus. They don't know what they're missing.

2. **Creating a little margin in your life to allow your soul room to breathe:** You can't just keep slogging on; you have to make room for recovery and resilience. A few evenings each week where you aren't doing anything. A day off now and then. But it can begin with five to ten minutes, morning and evening. (Here again, "30 Days to Resilient"—free within the One Minute Pause app—would be a simple way to start this practice.)

Notes

GROUP DISCUSSION

Take a few minutes to go through the following questions with your group.

1. In the opening adventure story, when the six men on a log raft approach their greatest peril yet—twenty-foot breakers pounding them into a jagged barrier reef—all they can think is: "Hold on, hold on, hold, hold, hold!" Have you ever had a situation where all you could do was just hold on? Would you share it with the group?

2. Where do you most struggle with divided allegiances? Why does this particular issue have such a pull on you?

3. Do you believe we are living at the end of the age? What are you basing your opinion on?

4. What stood out to you most from the passage in *Kon-Tiki*? Why?

5. As we near the end of this study on resilience, what supernatural grace, story, or teaching was especially significant to you? How will it impact your life going forward?

6. To weather the coming storm, you need a plan. Although it may not be fully developed yet, what are one or two components of your plan?

CLOSING PRAYER

Giving Your Eden Heart to Jesus

As we enter into this final prayer time, let's pray back through the things we have learned in these five sessions. Let's ask for supernatural resilience once again.

If you're doing this study with a group, ask someone to read this closing prayer aloud. If you are going through this on your own, find a quiet space where you can speak the words aloud.

Father, Jesus, Holy Spirit, I give my Eden heart to you, Lord, and you alone. I'm so filled with longing, Lord, for things to be good again. I just want things to be beautiful. I just want people to love one another. I want this turmoil to be over. I want evil to stop.

Jesus, catch my Eden heart. I put my hope in the restoration of Eden when you return. I give my heart to you and your return. You are the only safe place. There is only one Eden. I give my heart to the true and only Eden, which you will restore when you return.

I treasure you above all things. I now ask for the strength that prevails, the strength to escape the madness of this world. The supernatural strength that rises up from Jesus Christ who dwells within me. I ask for strength in my mental life, strength of heart, strength in my emotions, strength of will. I am your temple, Lord—fill your temple with your Glory, your radiant presence. Let your Glory shield me from all Desolation in the world.

I pray to be completely converted. I give you the unconverted places in me. I pray for the salvation that is truly salvation, which is to be fully inhabited by Christ. I give my attention to you deep within me; teach me to commune with you Lord, where you live in my inmost being.

God, I choose you. I choose single-heartedness. I give my Eden heart to you, Jesus. I turn my back on this world and I choose you. Fill me with a supernatural resilience for this hour. In your mighty name I pray.

> To go deeper, try the program
> "30 Days to Resilient"—free within the
> One Minute Pause App.

FINAL PERSONAL STUDY

In this section, you're invited to further explore the material in *Resilient*. If you haven't already done so, read chapter 10, "Hold On!," in the book at this time. Each day's study in this section offers a short reading from the book along with reflection questions designed to take you deeper into the themes of the study. Journal or just jot a few thoughts after each question. Since this is the final session, these final five days are specifically for your personal growth and private reflection.

Day One: THE ENEMY'S SNARE

The 2020 pandemic and what followed was an apocalypse—which means a "revealing," or exposing. Among all that has been revealed, the most concerning is our divided allegiances.

The fear that overcame all of us in varying degrees revealed that our security was not as firmly established in Christ as we thought. The grasping for life to be good again revealed that our hope was not exactly centered in Christ either. Now the Falling Away is revealing how deep our disappointments with God actually run, how easily these shallow roots can be upended.

Through the preceding sessions, I've described a number of the effects of the global trauma on me—my compulsive buying, the fixing up of our home, the little comforts I've turned to. I'm also having the most interesting experience: memories keep coming up of goodness long past. I'm remembering moments from trips taken years ago and experiencing sweet nostalgia from my childhood. I'm not one to reminisce much, but it's happening a good deal, almost unbidden—thinking of great times gone by and wondering how to get them back again.

Was this happening to Lot's wife as she ran across the plain?

Throughout God's long, tempestuous love affair with the human race recorded in both Testaments, the central dilemma has always been, and will always be, double-mindedness. The lack of wholeheartedness. "These people honor me with their lips, but their hearts are far from me" (Matthew 15:8).

The real danger is when you seem to have secured your life again. You finally quit your job, you moved to a new place, you fell in love. Because of everything we've covered here—the trauma, the fear of deprivation, the utter relief of having life good again—your heart quietly says, *I'm good, I don't need anything now.* The thought of the return of Christ disappears like an early morning fog burned away by noon. Let some other generation deal with that.

> *Your love is like the morning mist,*
> *like the early dew that disappears.*
>
> — HOSEA 6:4

The snare the enemy set for our hearts was to afflict us, traumatize us, tempt us, and get our hearts to land in a place where we sigh, feel relief, and say, *I'm good. This is good.* Without God. A taste of the kingdom without the King.[41]

I. Have events such as the pandemic and its aftermath exposed divided allegiances within you that were perhaps there all along? If so, when and how was this revealed to you?

2. The central dilemma between God and the human race has always been, and will always be, our double-mindedness. Our lack of wholeheartedness. As Jesus said, "These people honor me with their lips, but their hearts are far from me" (Matthew 15:8). Where does your heart feel far from God right now?

3. The enemy often traumatizes us, tempts us, and then gets our hearts to land in a place where we sigh, feel relief, and say, *I'm good. This is good.* Without God. What currently feels like it holds the promise of deep life and joy—whether God shows up or not?

Day Two: WE ONLY *SORT OF* WANT GOD

During the spring and summer of 2020, Stasi found herself enjoying a new distraction. She spent hours and hours on her laptop, looking at cottages for sale in Ireland and Scotland. It was a lovely detachment from the crisis, and dreaming is actually good for the soul. Besides, we have a long history with those countries. They are part of our lineage, we have dear friends who live there, and we feel a missional pull to minister there. But what our *hearts* remember is idyllic moments we've shared there on vacation, the kind of holiday where everything is right and wonderful, and the world felt a million miles away.

Stasi's obsession began in the quarantines, but it has carried on. Because the longing for life to be good again is not subsiding; it is growing stronger in every human heart.

Just this morning she told me, "I found an estate for sale on the west coast of the Scottish Highlands. Near that little village we love. It has its own loch and streams!" I was kind of surprised this came up again, after all the soul-work we've done. We've walked through the practices in this book together, tending our recovery and resilience. *An estate in the highlands? My wife has lost her mind.* I was already dismissing it when she added, "There's red stag hunting and fly-fishing on the property!"

Suddenly I see it—the heathered hills sweeping up to craggy peaks. The cascading streams bubbling down through mossy meadows. The loch with a little boat drawn up on the pebbled beach. Sunlight sparkling on the ocean as the sun sinks into the west. A fire in the fireplace and a dram of single malt on the table in our little white house overlooking it all.

Quicker than any mental reflection, my heart did a one-eighty. *Done.* I was ready to cash in our retirement and buy the place, sell everything we have, leave our loved ones and work behind to go get our little slice of happiness and respite. *Let the world collapse, I don't care. I'm done with all this. When can we move?*

I'm standing in the kitchen on a fairly ordinary Saturday afternoon watching the ancient battle for the human heart play out in my soul. Because I'm stressed out and traumatized and I just want a break. I want life to be good.

Remember Lot's wife.

I shudder at how easily my heart can be divided. I do love God, I really do. I know you do too. The double-mindedness is revealed when we only *sort of* want God. Our longing for life to be good again becomes the test we hold up against God—if he seems to be helping, wonderful. We believe. If he doesn't, well . . . we're going to chase whatever we think will fill our longing and get back to God sometime down the road. Powerful, ancient forces are pulling us in that direction.[42]

I. Did this story of longing for a cottage in Ireland remind you of a time when you found yourself considering an over-the-top purchase or trip simply from a desire for life to be good again? How did your story play out?

2. How can your desire for life to be good again, if it comes from a divided heart, harken back to the tragic story of Lot's wife?

3. Although it may be hard to admit, what is a place in your heart right now where you only *sort of* want God? Can you see now the powerful, ancient forces trying to pull you in that direction?

Day Three: OUR FALSE EDENS

We are in such a vulnerable moment.

We must, we must, we must choose single-heartedness, where we desire Jesus above everything else—above all our other "lovers," our false Edens, our passing comforts.

If you want to become a wholehearted person, you must reach the point where happily, lovingly, you give absolutely everything over to God. You make Jesus your everything, your all-in-all. Not only is this the fulfillment of your heart's created destiny, it is also the source of all recovery and resilience. Nothing can be taken from you because you've already surrendered everything.

I love summer. It's Stasi's and my favorite time of year. But here in Colorado we're now deep in the transition to fall, and all of our beautiful flower baskets are going to die. We made our front porch a little Eden refuge this year, a lush botanical garden, and I feel the clock ticking. Something in me rises up in a desperate, *No!* I'm out there every day pruning, feeding, coaxing them along.

I noticed this morning that dry rot is creeping over my favorite hanging basket. And in another pot some pest is munching holes through every bloom. You can't hold on to things, friends; there's no looking back. It doesn't do any good, but it *can* do an enormous amount of harm. Remember Lot's wife.

You can't go back, especially at a time when God is moving things forward. He wants us to come along with him.

I give everything for your everything.

This is now my prayer.

I give everything for your everything.

A few friends of mine have very deep and special relationships with God. They hear from him, receive visions of the things he is doing on the earth. Recently one of them sent me an account of a vision he had of the actual scene-behind-the-scenes in this great hour. He did not know I was writing this book; he had not heard a word about this chapter. Yet this is what he sent:

During the battle at the end, many people lost their faith, like Lot's wife (Genesis 19:26). They walked away from holiness, turned, not seen clearly, and had essentially sided with the enemy. Right at the end. Sadly, very sadly, some just didn't make it—many of whom had been expected to right up to the end.[43]

1. "If you want to become a wholehearted person, you must reach the point where happily, lovingly, you give absolutely everything over to God." What is your initial reaction to that statement . . . and why?

2. Though it may be hard to give absolutely everything to God, once you do, nothing can be taken from you because you've already surrendered everything. What does that thought stir in your heart?

3. Especially in these turbulent times, we really can't hold on to things. Looking back doesn't do any good, but it *can* do an enormous amount of harm. Given that, what do you need to let go of now? Will you let go of it?

Day Four: OUR HEIGHTENED STATE OF LONGING

"But we are not like those who turn away from God to their own destruction. We are the faithful ones, whose souls will be saved" (Hebrews 10:39 NLT).

I wonder—could our heightened state of longing for things to be good again be far more than a response to trauma, chronic disappointment, and deprivation? Might it actually be pointing to something wonderful?

If the heavens are thrilling as they stage for the return of Christ, if the battle on earth is raging, if Christ himself is standing at the door—wouldn't our hearts somehow recognize it? He who is our heart of hearts, our deepest desire, and most sincere longing, is drawing near—nearer than ever before. This would be especially moving for those in whom Christ dwells. Maybe—just maybe—our hearts are responding to the imminent return of Jesus while our rational minds continue to dismiss the thought.

When the moon comes closest to the earth in its orbital swing—what is called the perigee of the moon—the gravitational pull on the earth is strongest. A few times each year, the perigee coincides with a full moon and the gravitational attraction is strong indeed, causing tidal upheaval and flooding. Many scientists believe that the moon was once a part of the earth, that it broke away during a catastrophic event and now orbits like an estranged lover. When it draws near, the earth feels its presence deeply.[44]

Wouldn't our hearts do the same?

This is the greatest love story ever told, the Sacred Romance. As the Hero approaches from his long sojourn, his bride knows in her heart that he's coming—like the lovers in the song who can feel each other's heartbeat "for a thousand miles."[45]

Compasses are known to behave strangely as they near magnetic north. A compass induced to start spinning while close to what has pulled it all these years will continue spinning until something slows and stops it.[46] Perhaps all this crazy and erratic human behavior in this hour might indicate the loss of bearing that comes when something strong begins to overwhelm our *internal* compasses. Someone is approaching.

What sort of magnetic pull would the approach of our Lord and Master have on the hearts that love him?

Stasi and I have two golden retrievers. I sometimes call them "lampreys," because they cling to us whenever we're around. If we get up and move to another room, they will always get up and follow, every time, then lie happily again at our feet (as they are doing right now while I write this). Whenever we leave the house, they are desolate, and whenever Stasi or I draw near to home, as we are pulling into the neighborhood but several houses away, our goldens will wake up, even from a deep nap, run to the garage door, and stand there wagging their happy tails. They know when their masters are approaching.

I wonder if our hearts are doing the same thing. There is an ache, awakening down in the depths of our hearts that nothing else can assuage.[47]

1. Have you considered that our heightened state of longing for things to be good again may be far more than a response to trauma, chronic disappointment, and deprivation? If so, what do you sense is really going on?

2. If your heightened state of longing for things to be good again is actually your heart responding to the imminent return of Jesus, would that interpretation help you re-think those longings . . . and how to fulfill them?

3. Do you personally sense the magnetic pull in your heart signaling the approach of our Lord and Master? If so, how does that bolster your resilience?

Day Five: HOLD ON!

Beneath the surface of our busy and besieged lives, our Eden hearts are always searching for home. And isn't it striking that the most dangerous part of most journeys come right at the end of the survival story? Just like ours. In the adventure story of the six men on the raft, they made it through because they didn't let go. They acted like survivors till the end; they held on.

We are so close, friends. Guaranteed. There's no need to fear or grasp or look back.

So what shall we do?

We take the things in this study seriously. We rearrange our lives to center around God, so that we might take hold of the strength that prevails. We handle our recovery and resilience as seriously as any survivor would. We have a plan for going forward. And then we hold on to it!

We remember Lot's wife, as our Lord commanded. Every time our hearts are tempted to look back, we redouble our love for Jesus, knowing that strong, dark currents are trying to pull us away. We take hold of the supernatural graces! We give everything for his everything, diving deep in our innermost being to find the God who gives us resilience.

His resilience will not fail us.

Soon we will be laughing and singing with healed hearts as we walk with Jesus in a completely healed world.[48]

1. Your Eden heart is searching for home. What reminders can you keep before you to remember to "hold on" no matter how hopeless things appear in this world?

2. What is one practical way you can rearrange your life to center more around God?

3. Which supernatural grace would prove a rescue for your heart if you spent additional time in it for the next several days or weeks? Will you commit to doing so?

WHERE DO YOU GO FROM HERE?

Well done! You've completed this study. Yet there is so much more. The *Resilient* book has many more chapters that we could not include in these five sessions (chapters 2, 3, 5, 7, and 9). We hope you'll take time to read *Resilient* cover to cover—or perhaps listen to the book on audio for an entirely new experience. It includes a wealth of bonus content from John.

Once again, we also encourage you to get "30 Days to Resilient"—it is free within the One Minute Pause app and provides a beautiful morning and evening guided experience through the concepts introduced here. From there, you can continue the journey at www.wildatheart.org where you'll find weekly podcasts, a wealth of free audio and video resources, event updates, and more.

LEADER'S GUIDE

Thank you for your willingness to lead your group through *Resilient: Restoring Your Weary Soul in These Turbulent Times.* The rewards of leading are different from the rewards of participating, and we hope you find your own walk with Jesus deepened by this experience. This leader's guide will give you some tips on how to prepare for your time together and facilitate a meaningful experience for your group members.

WHAT DOES IT TAKE TO LEAD THIS STUDY?

Get together and watch God show up. Seriously, that's the basics of how a small group works. Gather several people together who have a hunger for God, want to learn how to get their lives back, and are willing to be open and honest with God and themselves. The Lord will honor this every time and show up in the group. You don't have to be a pastor, priest, theologian, or counselor to lead a group through this study. Just invite people over, watch the video, and talk about it. All you need is a willing heart, a little courage, and God will do the rest. Really.

HOW THIS STUDY WORKS

As the group leader, you will want to make sure everyone in your group has a copy of this study guide and access to the videos, which are available for them to view at any time by following the instructions printed on the inside front cover. (The group members will also want to have a copy of the *Resilient* book if they are doing the recommended readings for each session.) It works best if you can get the guides (and books) to your group *before* the first meeting. That way, everyone can read the material in the book ahead of time and be prepared to watch the first video session together.

This series is presented in five video sessions, with each session ranging from approximately seventeen to twenty-six minutes in length. Each week, you will meet together to watch the video and discuss the session. This series can also be used in classroom settings, such as Sunday school classes, though you may need to modify the discussion time depending on the size of the class. You could even use the video as sessions for a special prayer retreat.

Basically, each week you will: (1) discuss the opening Core Scripture questions, (2) watch the video sessions, (3) talk about them, and then (4) reflect on what you have learned by completing the between-sessions activities. That's it!

A FEW TIPS FOR LEADING A GROUP

The setting really matters. If you can choose to meet in a living room over a conference room in a church, do it. Pick an environment that's conducive to people relaxing and getting real. Remember the enemy likes to distract us when it comes to seeking God, so do what you can to remove these obstacles from your group (silence cell phones, limit background noise, no texting). Set the chairs or couches in a circle to prevent having a "classroom" feel.

Have some refreshments! Coffee and water will do; cookies and snacks are even better. People tend to be nervous when they join a new group, so if you can give them something to hold onto (like a warm mug of coffee), they will relax a lot more. It's human nature.

Good equipment is important. Meet where you can watch the video sessions on a screen big enough for everyone to see and enjoy. Get or borrow the best gear you can. Also, be sure to test your media equipment ahead of time to make sure everything is in working condition. This way, if something isn't working, you can fix it or make other arrangements before the meeting begins. (You'll be amazed at how the enemy will try to mess things up for you!)

Be honest. Remember that your honesty will set the tone for your time together. Be willing to answer questions personally, as this will set the pace for the length of your group members' responses and will make others more comfortable in sharing.

Stick to the schedule. Strive to begin and end at the same time each week. The people in your group are busy, and if they can trust you to be a good steward of their time, they will be more willing to come back each week. Of course, you want to be open to the work God is doing, and at times you may want to *linger* in prayer or discussion. Remember the clock serves *you*;

your group doesn't serve the clock. But work to respect the group's time, especially when it comes to limiting the discussion times.

Don't be afraid of silence or emotion. Welcome awkward moments. The material presented during this study will challenge the group members to reconsider some of their beliefs and compel them to make the necessary changes in their lives. Don't be afraid to ease into the material with the group.

Don't dominate the conversation. Even though you are the leader, you are also a member of this small group. So don't steamroll over others in an attempt to lead—and don't let anyone else in the group do so either.

Prepare for your meeting. Watch the video for the meeting ahead of time. Although it may feel a bit like cheating because you'll know what's coming, you will be better prepared for what the session might stir in the hearts of your group members. Also be sure to review the material in this guide and spend some time in prayer. In fact, the *most important* thing you can do is simply pray ahead of time each week:

Lord Jesus, come and rule this time. Let your Spirit fill this place. Bring your kingdom here. Take us right to the things we really need to talk about and rescue us from every distraction. Show us the heart of the Father. Meet each person here. Give us your grace and love for one another. In your name I pray.

Make sure your group members are prepared. Before the first meeting, secure enough copies of the study guide for each member. Have these ready and on hand for the first meeting, or make sure the participants have purchased them. Send out a reminder email or a text a couple of days before the meeting to make sure folks don't forget about it.

AS YOU GATHER

You will find the following counsel to be especially helpful when you meet for the first time as a group. I offer these comments in the spirit of "here is what I would do if I were leading a group through this study."

First, as the group gathers, start your time with introductions if people don't know each other. Begin with yourself and share your name, how long you've been a follower of Christ, if you have a spouse and/or children, and what you want to learn most from this study. Going first will put the group more at ease.

After the introductions, go through the Core Scripture section as you have time. Then jump right into watching the video teaching, as this will help get things started on a strong note. In the following weeks, you may want to start by allowing folks to catch up a little with some "how are you?" kind of banter. Too much of this burns up your meeting time, but you have to allow some room for it because it helps build relationships among the group members.

Note that each group will have its own personality and dynamics. Typically, people will hold back the first week or two until they feel the group is "safe." Then they will begin to share. Again, don't let it throw you if your group seems a bit awkward at first. Of course, some people *never* want to talk, so you'll need to coax them out as time goes on. But let it go the first week.

INSIGHT FOR DISCUSSION

If the group members are in any way open to talking about their lives as it relates to this material, you will likely *not* have enough time for every question suggested in this study guide. That's okay! Pick the questions ahead of time that you know you definitely want to cover, just in case you end up only having time to discuss a few of them.

You set the tone for the group. Your honesty and vulnerability during discussion times will tell them what they can share. How *long* you talk will give them an example of how long they should respond. So give some thought to what stories or insights from your own work in the study guide you want to highlight.

WARNING: The greatest temptation for most small group leaders is to add to the video teaching with a little "teaching session" of their own. This is unhelpful for three reasons:

1. The discussion time will be the richest time during your meeting. The video sessions have been intentionally kept short so you can have plenty of time for discussion. If you add to the teaching, you sacrifice this precious time.

2. You don't want your group members *teaching, lecturing,* or *correcting* one another. The group members are all at a different

place in their spiritual journey. If you set a tone by teaching, the group will feel like they have the freedom to teach one another. That can be disastrous for group dynamics.

3. The participants will be watching the video teachings during your group time and exploring the topics covered in more detail by completing the between-sessions activities. They don't need more content! What they want is a chance to talk and process their own lives in light of all they have taken in.

A STRONG CLOSE

Some of the best learning times will take place after the group time as God brings new insights to the participants during the week. Encourage group members to write down any questions they have as work through the between-sessions exercises. Make sure they know you are available for them as they explore the material. Finally, make sure you close your time by praying together—either by following the suggested prompts or coming up with your own closing prayers. Ask two or three people to pray, inviting God to fill your group and lead each person during this study.

Thanks again for taking the time to lead your group. May God reward your efforts and dedication by replenishing your reserves with his supernatural resilience.

ENDNOTES

1. Laurence Gonzales, *Deep Survival: Who Lives, Who Dies, and Why* (New York: W.W. Norton, 2017), 120.
2. Ed Yong, "What Happens When Americans Can Finally Exhale: The Pandemic's Mental Wounds Are Still Wide Open," *Atlantic*, May 20, 2021, https://www.theatlantic.com/health/archive/2021/05/pandemic-trauma-summer/618934/.
3. *Strong's Concordance*, s.v. "2729. *katischuó*," Bible Hub, accessed November 20, 2021, https://biblehub.com/greek/2729.htm.
4. Paulo Coelho, *The Alchemist*, trans. Alan R. Clarke (New York: HarperOne, 1993), 116
5. John Eldredge, *Resilient* (Nashville, TN: Nelson Books, 2022), ix–xii.
6. John Eldredge, *Resilient* (Nashville, TN: Nelson Books, 2022), 1–2, 4–5.
7. Dan B. Allender and Cathy Loerzel, *Redeeming Heartache: How Past Suffering Reveals Our True Calling* (Grand Rapids, MI: Zondervan, 2021).
8. Dana Rose Garfin, E. Alison Holman, and Roxane Cohen Silver, "Cumulative Exposure to Prior Collective Trauma and Acute Stress Responses to the Boston Marathon Bombings," *Psychological Science* 26, no. 6 (2015): 675–83, doi.org/10.1177/0956797614561043.
9. For the full story, see Edward Dolnick, *Down the Great Unknown: John Wesley Powell's 1869 Journey of Discovery and Tragedy Through the Grand Canyon* (New York: HarperCollins, 2001).
10. John Eldredge, *Resilient* (Nashville, TN: Nelson Books, 2022), 6–9.
11. "How Many Israelites Left Egypt in the Exodus?," Got Questions, accessed November 19, 2021, https://www.gotquestions.org/Israelites-exodus.html.

12. John Eldredge, *Resilient* (Nashville, TN: Nelson Books, 2022), 10–11.

13. Richard Gunderman, "For the Young Doctor About to Burn Out," *Atlantic*, February 21, 2014, http://www.theatlantic.com/health /archive/2014/02/for-the-young-doctor-about-to-burn-out/284005/.

14. John Eldredge, *Resilient* (Nashville, TN: Nelson Books, 2022), 13–15.

15. John Eldredge, *Resilient* (Nashville, TN: Nelson Books, 2022), 57–59.

16. John Eldredge, *Resilient* (Nashville, TN: Nelson Books, 2022), 59–61.

17. To explore the truth that the Christian is the temple of God, go to www.bibleproject.com and search their great resources on "temple." The more you understand the truth of this, the more you will be able to receive God's glory in you.

18. This may help some Christians understand the nearness of the last days if they have until now believed that the Jewish temple in Jerusalem needed to be rebuilt and the sacrificial system reinstated for the Abomination to do his thing. In the new covenant period, the location of the temple clearly shifts to the human heart. It's something to consider. But you don't need to accept this as a possible interpretation to realize that we need to strengthen our hearts against our enemy, especially in trying times.

19. John Eldredge, *Resilient* (Nashville, TN: Nelson Books, 2022), 61–63.

20. Jennifer K. Logue et al., "Sequelae in Adults at 6 Months After COVID-19 Infection," *JAMA Network Open* 4, no 2 (February 19, 2021), https://jamanetwork.com/journals/jamanetworkopen/full article/2776560.

21. Ed Yong, "What Happens When Americans Can Finally Exhale: The Pandemic's Mental Wounds Are Still Wide Open," *Atlantic*, May 20, 2021, https://www.theatlantic.com/health/archive/2021/05 /pandemic-trauma-summer/618934/.

22. John Eldredge, *Resilient* (Nashville, TN: Nelson Books, 2022), 64–65.

23. John Eldredge, *Resilient* (Nashville, TN: Nelson Books, 2022), 65–69.

24. John Eldredge, *Resilient* (Nashville, TN: Nelson Books, 2022), 95–96.

25. Walter Hooper, "Preface," *God in the Dock: Essays on Theology and Ethics* (1970; repr., Cambridge: William B. Eerdmans, 2014), xiv.

26. John Eldredge, *Resilient* (Nashville, TN: Nelson Books, 2022), 96–97.

27. Theodore Roosevelt, *Hunting Trips of a Ranchman and the Wilderness Hunter* (1885; repr., New York: The Modern Library, 1996), 436–37.

28. John Eldredge, *Resilient* (Nashville, TN: Nelson Books, 2022), 97–99.

29. John Eldredge, *Resilient* (Nashville, TN: Nelson Books, 2022), 101–105.

30. George MacDonald, *Unspoken Sermons Series I, II, and III* (1867; repr., New York: Start Publishing, 2012), 167.

31. John Eldredge, *Resilient* (Nashville, TN: Nelson Books, 2022), 105–106.

32. Nicholas Carr, *The Shallows: What the Internet Is Doing to Our Brains* (New York: W. W. Norton, 2010).

33. John Eldredge, *Resilient* (Nashville, TN: Nelson Books, 2022), 137–140.

34. Theophan the Recluse, quoted in *The Art of Prayer: An Orthodox Anthology,* comp. Igumen Chariton of Valamo, trans. E. Kadloubovsky and E. M. Palmer, ed. Timothy Ware (London: Faber and Faber, 1966), 110.

35. John Eldredge, *Resilient* (Nashville, TN: Nelson Books, 2022), 140–142.

36. John Eldredge, *Get Your Life Back* (Nashville, TN: Nelson Books, 2020), 16.

37. John Eldredge, *Get Your Life Back* (Nashville, TN: Nelson Books, 2020), 24–25.

38. John Eldredge, *Resilient* (Nashville, TN: Nelson Books, 2022), 142–145.

39. John Eldredge, *Resilient* (Nashville, TN: Nelson Books, 2022), 145–146.

40. John Eldredge, *Resilient* (Nashville, TN: Nelson Books, 2022), 147–149.

41. John Eldredge, *Resilient* (Nashville, TN: Nelson Books, 2022), 193–195.

42. John Eldredge, *Resilient* (Nashville, TN: Nelson Books, 2022), 195–197.

43. John Eldredge, *Resilient* (Nashville, TN: Nelson Books, 2022), 121, 197–199.

44. NOAA, "What Is a Perigean Spring Tide?," National Oceanic and Atmospheric Administration, last updated February 26, 2021, https://oceanservice.noaa.gov/facts/perigean-spring-tide.html; "Moon Facts," National Geographic, July 16, 2004, https://www.nationalgeographic.com/science/article/moon-facts.

45. Van Morrison, vocalist, "Crazy Love," by Van Morrison, recorded 1969, track 3 on *Moondance*, Warner Brothers, 33 $1/3$ rpm, 2:34.

46. "What Happens When a Compass Is Taken to the Site of Magnetic Pole of Earth?," Physics Stack Exchange, August 13, 2015,

https://physics.stackexchange.com/questions/200152/what-happens
-when-a-compass-is-taken-to-the-site-of-magnetic-pole-of-earth.

47. John Eldredge, *Resilient* (Nashville, TN: Nelson Books, 2022), 199–202.

48. John Eldredge, *Resilient* (Nashville, TN: Nelson Books, 2022), 205–206.

COMPANION BOOK
TO ENRICH YOUR
STUDY EXPERIENCE

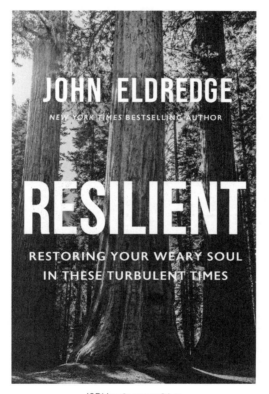

ISBN 9781400208647

Available wherever books are sold

NELSON
BOOKS

An Imprint of Thomas Nelson

Experience
"30 Days to Resilient"
in the **Pause App**.

"I've developed a simple plan to help you become resilient. It's the beginning of a new way of living. Your soul is going to thank you."

PauseApp.com

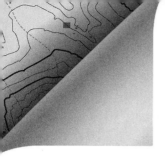

Finishing this study is only the beginning.

Continue your journey at
WildAtHeart.org

Weekly Podcasts

Video & Audio Resources

Prayers We Pray

Live Events

Download the **Wild at Heart App**.

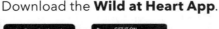

JOHN ELDREDGE
WILD *AT* HEART
Podcast

Wild at Heart offers weekly podcast
conversations with John Eldredge
and his team. It's free. It's powerful.
And it's better when you're in the
conversation with us.

ALSO AVAILABLE FROM
JOHN ELDREDGE

Study Guide
9780310097020

Video Study
9780310097037

Available now at your favorite bookstore,
or streaming video on StudyGateway.com.

HarperChristian Resources

ALSO AVAILABLE FROM
JOHN ELDREDGE

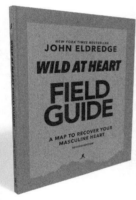  

Field Guide
9780310135647

Study Guide
9780310129103

DVD + Streaming Access
9780310129127

Available now at your favorite bookstore,
or streaming video on StudyGateway.com.

(H) Harper*Christian* Resources

ALSO AVAILABLE FROM
JOHN ELDREDGE

Study Guide

9780310682165

Video Study

9780310087656

Available now at your favorite bookstore, or streaming video on StudyGateway.com.

HarperChristian Resources

ALSO AVAILABLE FROM
JOHN ELDREDGE

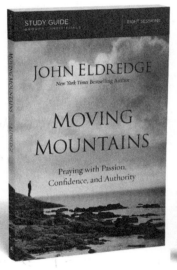
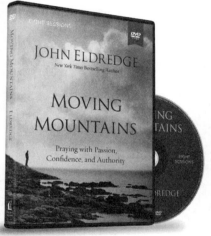

Study Guide
9780718038496

Video Study
9780718038526

Available now at your favorite bookstore,
or streaming video on StudyGateway.com.

(H) Harper*Christian* Resources

From the Publisher

GREAT STUDIES

ARE EVEN BETTER WHEN THEY'RE SHARED!

Help others find this study:

- Post a review at your favorite online bookseller.

- Post a picture on a social media account and share why you enjoyed it.

- Send a note to a friend who would also love it—or, better yet, go through it with them!

Thanks for helping others grow their faith!

Have you been
~~to~~ submitting all
these expense
~~&~~ receipts to
Accounting?
They want them
with in 3 days
of purchase.

ɩ Could be anyone farting
Lots of butts in here